Democratic Objectivecracy

Do You Want
Real
Democracy?

Bernardo De Urquidi

Table of Contents

From the writer to the reader

Thank you for reading this book. I hope it helps and motivates you to question the status quo, to develop your own ideas and opinions, to debate those opinions with me and with other people. I hope it helps you develop your own cause and the ideals for which you will strive and fight for, and I hope it helps you develop your own tools with which to fight for your own ideals.

This book is written in an unusual way, because my intention is not to tell you what to think, or just to convey ideas. My intention is to prompt you to analyze, evaluate, and judge the ideas presented in this book and that constitute your world view; that you analyze my arguments and judge whether they convince you or not, if you have counter arguments, if you have better ideas and if you can identify how the ideas we discuss are applied in the world and affect your life. The purpose of doing this is to help you develop your own ideas, arguments, even feelings on the subject of democracy, the distribution of power and the different ways in which we can organize ourselves as human beings. By the end of the book, I hope you will have developed your own position regarding power, democracy, freedoms, and social organization, and hopefully, because it is yours, you will defend and promote it.

To achieve this purpose, the book stops constantly to ask you to reflect on an idea or argument and to write your opinion or practical examples of what the book presents in theory. In this book there are no rhetorical questions, every question is meant for you to stop, reflect, and write an answer. Ideally, you will approach this book as if it were a conversation, a friendly debate in which you receive ideas, analyze them, and develop your own opinions. When you finish this book, I hope it contains as many of your thoughts, and writings as mine.

Thank you for taking this journey of reflection and development with me and I hope that soon we can take the journey to transform our societies; I hope that soon we can build free societies where we can collaborate freely.

Book Sections

This book is divided into 5 sections:

Section 1: What is the problem? In this section we will analyze and judge the system by which almost all developed and developing countries, at the beginning of the 21st century, are organized and governed, or pretend to be governed: Electoral Representative Democracy.

Section 2: How does it affect me? In this section, we will analyze the relationship of the individual with his circumstances and how our specific type of social organization currently determines or influences all the circumstances in which each human being develops, lives, and confronts.

Section 3: The other political systems. In this section we will analyze, evaluate, and judge the most important systems of social and political organization, from monarchies and dictatorships to direct democracy and sortition democracy.

Section 4: Democratic Objectivecracy. In this section, we will propose a new system of social and political organization, which is both democratic and efficient, and through which a free society of free human beings who strive and collaborate to achieve common objectives can be developed.

Section 5: Recommendations for a Democratic Objectivecracy. In this section, we will analyze some recommendations on ideas and topics that could affect the organization of a society that wishes to organize itself with the system of Democratic Objectivecracy. In addition, we explore some steps we can take to start the transition from the current system to the new one.

SECTION 1

What is the problem?

You are not free because your country is governed through the system called "Electoral Representative Democracy."

Electoral representative democracy is not a truly democratic system, it concentrates all the power in society in a few hands, and it is also an inefficient system that polarizes and divides society.

Under this system, the elected politicians have the power to control, modify, or influence the circumstances in which you live, and therefore, they control, modify, or influence the opportunities available to you, your freedoms, your civic duties, your economy, your security, your health, the impact your society has on the environment, etc. In this system, power is concentrated in a few hands.

In this system, you have the freedom to do what you want with the options, possibilities, and freedoms your circumstances generate; but your circumstances are influenced, modified, or determined by the elected politicians.

If others have the power to influence, modify, or determine the circumstances that generate the opportunities, possibilities, and freedoms you have, you are not free and the master of your own destiny.

CHAPTER 1

Democracy

What is democracy?

Democracy literally means government by the people. The word comes from the Greek "demos" which means people, and "kratia" which means government. That is, the people govern themselves. The "people" is composed of all citizens who are members of society. 1

Democracy is the system of social organization where each citizen maintains his freedom, and together with other citizens, participates in the decision-making process on matters that affect them and their society. Democracy is the system of government that affirms that the objectives, terms, and conditions and projects of the social contract must be freely agreed upon and accepted by all the citizens of a society. Democracy is the form of government in which all citizens participate with equal power to determine what is allowed, what is prohibited, what is encouraged, what is discouraged, and the objectives and projects of society as a whole. It is the form of government that determines the equality of rights for absolutely all of its citizens.

Democracy is the system in which citizens are not governed by others, but citizens govern themselves. This implies that there is no group that subdues, threatens, oppresses, or forces them to be part of society. There is no group or person that forces them to submit to a social contract in which others decide the objectives, terms, and conditions of the social contract. There is no group or person that decides and unilaterally influences the circumstances in which each citizen lives and develops. No one group or person who decides what freedoms, opportunities, and possibilities every citizen will have. There is no group or person who decides what the social hierarchy is and who occupies what position and how much power it has, or they have over the citizens or the circumstances in which the citizens live. In a Democracy, no one person or group has the power to impose a decision or circumstances over the other citizens.

In a democratic system, citizens choose the freedoms and the type of power that they limit and restrict, in order to be part of a society that protects and enhances their freedoms and generates new opportunities and possibilities for them. While in a tyranny, the system or the rulers dictate what freedoms each person may or may not have, what actions must be taken to remain "alive" and "free" within the imposed limits, and what benefits will be obtained in return. In a democracy, citizens decide what freedoms they sacrifice and what activities they will carry out to develop and be part of a society that offers them the benefits they have chosen.

While in a dictatorship or a tyranny all the political power of a society is concentrated in a few hands, in a democracy power is distributed equally and evenly among all the citizens. All the citizens have the same power and opportunity to determine the direction of the society and the circumstances in which they live.

A democratic system organizes citizens so that they can govern themselves. There are many types of social systems that are called democratic; some of them, like electoral representative democracy, are not actually democratic; others, such as direct democracy and sortition democracy are, in fact, democratic but are not very efficient or don't work in large societies. Through this book, we will evaluate where each political system distributes or concentrates power, who makes the decisions that affect every citizen's lives, and their efficiency.

CHAPTER 2

Electoral Representative Democracy

Government by the elected representatives.

Electoral Representative Democracy has been promoted as the only true form of democracy in the entire world since the establishment of the first French Republic after the revolution. Equating elective representation with democracy was reinforced and promoted with the independence of the United States of America and every other American country. From then until now, the word freedom has been linked to the word democracy, the word voting, and the word representative. Especially after the Second World War, the fall of most totalitarian states, and the independence of the colonies, the world and the movements of people seeking freedom in their societies, have moved towards electoral representative democracy under the false idea that this is the ultimate democratic and free system, that this is the best form of government; where free citizens can exercise control of their government and their lives, under the false idea that it is the most stable and effective form of democracy.

Little by little, this idea has been deteriorating. Little by little, we have come to realize that, in reality, electoral representative democracy is not democracy; that power is not in "the people", that citizens have no control over their society or government, that they are not free, that they do not really influence or determine their own circumstances. Some have perceived that something is wrong with the governments that rule over us, and they have immediately pointed to politicians, institutions, parties, and government officials and have blamed them for the problem.

"That politician and that party is corrupt!
That politician is ignorant!
That politician and that party do not work for us!
That politician and that party are oppressors!
Society and the country are in bad shape, and it is the politicians' and the parties' fault!"

This perspective has led thousands and millions to protest on the streets, to demonstrate against governments, to form new parties, to vote for non-politicians, for people outside the "political establishment", outside the "political class", for "populists" who speak out against traditional politicians and who promise to work for the interests of the "people". However, the problems generated by the "elected representatives and rulers" are not solved with another representative or ruler with better qualities, more honest, more intelligent, or with the correct ideology. The problems we are facing as a society are the product of the system itself. Corrupt and bad political parties and politicians only exacerbate and make the problems more visible. But even if every politician and political party were to be 100% honest, intelligent, capable, and they sought with complete honesty their conception of the 'common good', the system of electoral representation will still not be democratic, it will remain oppressive, polarizing, and divisive. This will not change by changing the party or the politician, this will only change by completely changing the system.

But before talking about new systems, let's talk about the problems of electoral representative democracy.

Basically, electoral representative democracy is a system in which citizens elect one or more representatives and give them the power to rule over them, to govern them, or to administer public affairs for a limited period of time. The practical application of this simple idea has varied throughout history and now varies according to the country in which it is applied. The United States, Mexico, France, and

Germany apply electoral representative democracy in different ways, but each country follows the basic principle that the people must be governed by representatives elected by the citizens.

In theory, when choosing a representative, the citizen chooses someone who takes charge and is responsible for the public life of the country. This involves making decisions and executing actions that affect the lives and circumstances of all citizens. This implies that the citizen will not participate in the decision-making process and the execution of actions that will affect his life. Instead, in theory, the representative dedicates all his time, effort, and intellectual capacity to making decisions according to the interests of his electorate.

A democratic system organizes people so that they can govern themselves. An elective representative system, organises people so that they can choose who will govern them.

Without going into detail about the practical ways in which electoral representative democracy is applied in each country, even in its general concept, in its purest, theoretical, simplest, and abstract form, we can find several reasons why it is not a truly democratic system.

Electoral representative democracy is not a democratic system for the following reasons:

Reason 1: Representatives of some, rulers of all.

The first defect of electoral representative democracy is that the representatives who rule over all are not elected by all citizens. That is, in an election, there is a winner, and one or more losers, and power is in the hands of the winning representative. The representative is not elected by all citizens and does not need the support of all citizens to stay in power. Even when the elected representative is honest, intelligent, capable, and seldom makes mistakes, the fact that he was voted into power by only a part of the population means he does not represent the entire population.

The representative will represent only those who voted for him, those who elected him. If a representative really represents his electorate, then he cannot represent the electorate that voted for the opposition. This implies that the citizen who voted for the losing candidate is not represented by the winner of the election, and therefore not represented in government.

Electoral representative democracy is the government of the representative over those who voted for him, who he supposedly represents, and over those who did not vote for him and who he does not represent. If the ideological differences between political parties and candidates are not very large then the best scenario is that the elected official will govern without representing everyone. If the candidates' ideological positions are opposite and the interests of their electorate are opposite to each other, then the winning representative, in order to represent those who voted for him, will have to work against the interests, ideologies, and beliefs of those who did not vote for him. This means that in a functional electoral representative democracy, the representative can govern in favor of the interests of the electors that voted for him, and against the interests of those that did not.

In an electoral representative democracy, the elected official can represent his voters and ignore or oppress those who did not vote for him. In a representative democracy, those who voted for the losing candidate are governed, in every respect, by the representatives of those who did win. The representatives of the winners have the power to choose the direction of society, the objective towards which they are directed, the laws that establish what is allowed, what is prohibited, what is encouraged and what is discouraged in the society; and through the laws and actions the government undertakes, it generates the circumstances in which each person lives, develops, and confronts.

The representatives of the "winners" will be able to decide, or will influence the physical and economic security of each member of society; they will determine or influence the education, entertainment, health, freedoms, opportunities, and possibilities of the members of society; they will determine or influence the impact that society will have on the environment, etc. The representatives will determine or impact the circumstances of all who live in the society according to the interests of those who voted for them. The moment a representative wins, those who did not vote for him are excluded from being part of the decision-making process that will determine and influence the society, the circumstances, the freedoms, the opportunities, and the obligations of everyone living in the society. When a group of people vote for a candidate that lost the election, the right to govern themselves is taken away from them and they are governed by the representatives of others. The electoral process determines who will have the right to be governed by their representative and who will be governed by the representative of other people.

In summary:

- Representatives are not elected by all citizens, therefore not all citizens are represented in government.

- Citizens whose candidate lost the election are governed by the representatives of the winers without being taken into consideration.

- Representatives can govern, legislate, or execute, taking into account the interests of the people who voted for them, and ignoring or working against the interests of those who did not vote for them.

- Representatives can represent their electorate and ignore or oppress those who did not vote for them.

- Those who lost the elections lose the right to be part of, or influence, the decision-making process, so they do not govern themselves.

- The electoral process determines who will have the right to be governed by the person they choose, and who will be governed by the representative of others.

Now is the time to stop and reflect. Can you think of practical examples for this theoretical critique? When the opposition, the candidate, or the party that you dislike the most wins, do you feel represented by your government? Are you afraid of the consequences that their actions may have on your life? Do you feel ignored or oppressed? When the party or candidate you dislike most wins, do you think and feel that you live in a democracy where you are part of the government? Do you think that the government and the power are really distributed equally among all citizens?

____

____

____

____

____

____

____

____

____

____

____

____

____

____

____

Reason 2: The polarization of society.

From the previous defect, another arises: the polarizing tendency of the electoral representative democracy system. The first consequence of not being a democratic system in which all share power and government, but a system in which power is in the hands of a few people, and all are governed by the representatives of some, is that elections become a process that determines who will be represented and who will be ignored or oppressed. Elections are not a process by which citizens come together to choose and build the future of their society, to choose their objectives, decide what is allowed and what is prohibited, the responsibilities and rights of each citizen, to decide the projects and the actions that all members of society will undertake together, and to decide the circumstances in which they want to live, the society they want to develop and how they will get there. The process of electing representatives determines who is represented and who is ignored or oppressed. Therefore, the victory of the representative of the other group or party has devastating consequences for the loser; because during the time that the others' representative governs, he or she will work without taking the loser into account, will work against their interests, or may even oppress the loser.

The citizens of an electoral representative democracy recognize in the candidate or voter of the other party a possible oppressor, turning that party and the opposite electorate into real enemies. This generates opposing groups in society that fight to govern everyone. Electoral representative democracy makes citizens enemies of one another, it divides them by warning them that the opposition wants to oppress them.

Since candidates do not need the approval and support of all citizens to gain, obtain, and maintain power, candidates can afford to directly condemn part of the population, usually a minority, or the ideas or ideologies of the opposing candidate and the citizens who support them. The candidate not only does not represent the interests of the entire population but can actively speak out against the interests of a certain part of the population. This incandescent, accusatory, condemning rhetoric and the vilification and demonization of one candidate towards another, their ideology and their supporters, has a polarizing effect on the electorate and therefore on the entire population, damaging the cohesive forces of the social fabric.

A group of citizens sees in a candidate their representative, or leader, and the champion of their cause, and in the other candidate an oppressive or threatening force. Therefore, the citizen will tend to see, as part of the oppressive or threatening force, any other citizen who supports the opposing candidate or his/her ideology.

This polarizing effect is even greater when political parties are established from which the candidates for representative are chosen. Because the gregarious sense of belonging and identity created by being a member of a group generates the idea and feeling that opposition to the party is a threat to oneself and to those who sympathize with the party's ideals. The parties represent certain interests of a sector of the population, so they are against the parties and the sector of the population that has other interests or opposing views and ideas. This opposition of representatives and interests is a continuous one, which does not end when the campaign and voting cycles end. The opposition is maintained all the time, therefore the parties and politicians are always accusing each other, generating a society with perpetual forces that divide and polarize the citizens. Even if the party or representative in power is not fighting against the interests of those who did not win the election, if the opposition party intends to win the next election they must create the perception that those who govern are not doing a good job and are oppressing society, generating the perception in the citizenry that, in effect, they are always being oppressed or attacked.

Electoral representative democracy generates the perception that the "other" is an enemy and therefore justifies that their opinions, concerns, desires, ideas, and proposals are not taken into account to establish the laws and circumstances in which everyone lives. In this system, citizens fight each other to give power to their representatives or leaders to govern and rule over everyone. This turns the election system into a process of choosing and legitimizing an oppressor.

In summary:

- The consequences of losing the elections are that the interests of those who lost are not taken into account during the government of the winners.

- Since candidates and representatives do not need all citizens to obtain and maintain power, they can attack opposing politicians and the sector of the population that supports other politicians. These attacks divide and polarize the population.

- Candidates and politicians can attack and speak up against the sector of the population that supports the opposing candidates. This pushes citizens to view each other as enemies.

- By attacking the other candidates, and the part of the population that supports them, politicians generate the perception among their sympathizers that the other candidates and their supporters are a personal threat or an enemy to their interests.

- Due to the fact that citizens perceive as enemies those who voted for the opposition, they can justify not taking their enemies into account and oppressing them during the time that their representative has power.

Now is the time to stop and reflect. Think about your perception and feelings towards the politicians of the parties that you dislike and towards those who vote for them. How do you see and what do you think of the politicians and political parties that you don't like? How do you perceive and what do you think of the people who usually vote for the political party that you dislike the most? How do people around you who are more polarized than you perceive those who vote for the political party they dislike? Do you think that if society is so polarized and power so concentrated in a few hands, a democracy can really function in which citizens are not oppressed? Do you think polarization is good or will bring positive results to your society? Do you think that the idea that the opposition or the "others" are enemies, stupid or bad is good for your society? Do you think that those who support the other party think so of you? Do you think there are people who think you are an enemy, an oppressor, a threat to their interests, or stupid for voting for whom you vote for?

____

____

____

____

____

____

____

____

Reason 3: Fear campaigns and representatives who do not represent anyone.

The combination of the previous flaws generates a system in which the elected officials do not necessarily have to represent their constituents, but to maintain power, it is sufficient for them to generate fear, resentment, or hatred towards the opposition. The candidate does not have to represent, he only needs to convince the electorate that the "OTHER" is a greater threat to their interests. It is not necessary for the elected official to carry out actions to support those who voted for him; it is enough to convince them that the opposition is worse, or that the opposition is an enemy. If this happens, the system does not comply with being democratic for any of its citizens. It is a system where a few, with the consent of a fearful section of the electorate, gain the power to govern everyone, without having to represent anyone.

In summary:

- As society polarizes, candidates or representatives can concentrate all their campaign efforts to generate feelings of resentment, fear, or hatred for the other candidates and the people that support them.

- A candidate may be elected, not because he/she represents the interests of his/her constituents, but because those who vote for him/her fear, resent, or hate the other candidates and the population they represent.

- If this happens, no one is represented, all are governed by those who could instigate more people to feel fear, resentment, or hatred towards the opposition.

Have you ever voted for the "least worst" or the "lesser of two evils"? Have you ever voted or thought about voting because you are afraid that the opposition will win? Or do you know people who do vote for the least worst or for fear of the other candidates? Do candidates often speak in ways that make you afraid of what might happen if the opposition wins? Do you think you live in a democracy if you are governed by "the least worst" or the "lesser of two evils"? Do you think you live in a democracy if you are afraid of what might happen if a candidate you dislike wins? Do you think you live in a democracy if someone can gain power only because he convinced many citizens to fear or hate another candidate and another group of citizens?

____

____

____

____

____

____

____

____

____

____

____

Reason 4: Personal criteria of the representatives.

In an electoral representative democracy, representatives maintain their own criteria and decide, legislate, and govern according to their own criteria and not that of their electorate; therefore, even if they do this with the best of intentions, when they are using their personal judgment they are not representing the citizens. When the representative decides, according to their own criteria and not according to what has been expressed by his constituents, then the representative is not representing anyone and the result is a system in which everyone is governed and no one is represented. It is a system in which a few who won election obtain the power to rule over everyone.

In summary:

- If a representative acts according to his personal criteria and not according to the criteria of those who voted for him, then he is not representing them.

- When officials govern, legislate, or execute according to their personal judgment, they are not representing anyone, and therefore citizens are governed and not represented.

Do you always feel represented by your representatives? Do you feel or think that the representatives work for your interests or according to what you consider to be the right thing to do? Do you think they work according to what most citizens consider to be the right thing to do? Do you think that if the representative can govern using personal criteria or his own ideas, which are not those of the electorate, he is really representing his electorate?

____
____
____
____
____
____
____
____
____
____
____
____
____

Reason 5: The representatives cannot represent their electorate in everything.

Even when a politician wishes to represent his electorate, his electorate are people, human beings, who are different from each other. It is implausible to think that all of a representative's represented have exactly the same interests and views in all areas of public and social life. The candidates and the political parties usually have within their proposals an amalgamation of ideas, proposals, objectives, and projects; and the electors choose the representative and the party because they agree with some of the representative's proposals, although they might be against some of their other proposals. Therefore, even when the representative acts according to his campaign promises, he will surely act against some of the interests of his electorate. By forcing citizens to choose a representative, they are forced to choose between candidates who represent them in some ways and do not represent them in some other ways. Therefore, in the best scenario, in an electoral representative democracy, those who govern represent their electorate in some respects, they do not represent them in every issue, and they do not represent at all those who voted for the opposition; this implies that they can work against some of the interests of those who voted for them and against all the interests of those who did not vote for them.

In summary:

- Each candidate presents several campaign proposals and promises. Voters may agree with some proposals and disagree with others. When choosing a representative, they choose a person who does not represent them in everything.

- The election winners represent those who voted for them on some issues, do not represent them on other issues, and do not represent at all those who did not vote for them.

Do the candidates you voted for represent you in everything? Have you voted for a representative who has something you like but many other things you dislike? Is your representative really someone who only represents you in some things and not in others? Do you vote for a candidate because he/she really represents you or because they have at least something you like while the opposition has more things you dislike?

____
____
____
____
____
____
____
____
____
____
____
____
____
____

Reason 6: The Representative's character flaws and deficiencies.

To the above-mentioned structural failures, to the failures that are part of or generated by the system itself and that have nothing to do with the individuals and human beings elected, we must add the character flaws, defects, and deficiencies of the elected representatives.

Because representatives, just like any other human, have many defects, deficiencies, limitations, desires, and personal ambitions. When choosing a representative, their vices, their traumas, their conscious and subconscious desires, their moral character, their personal perception of justice, and their ignorance are chosen. When choosing a representative, a person with limitations and shortcomings is chosen. The problem is not that representatives are not perfect or that they are human beings with vices, traumas, ignorance, and shortcomings, but that a lot of society's power is placed on their hands. These limitations and shortcomings will have repercussions for all the citizens of a country. If a flawed human being holds too much power in their hands, they will use that power in a flawed way. Politicians know this, that is why they hide their personal life and flaws form the public as much as posible, they try to present themselves as superior to the people to justify the power they hold over the people.

Who would trust a flawed human being with power over the government, the armies, the police, the taxation system, the judicial system, the environment, education and every other aspect of the circumstances in which they live?

In summary:

- The representatives are not perfect, they are human beings with defects, deficiencies, ignorance, trauma, vices, flaws, etc. Giving them a great amount of power over society means that they will inevitably make bad decisions and mistakes that will have repercussions for all members of society.

Can you think of a candidate, a ruler, a president, a legislator, etc. that you think is ignorant, stupid, or immoral? Have you ever voted for a candidate who later turned out to be incompetent? Have you voted for a candidate who turned out to be corrupt and immoral? Or have you seen how others vote for candidates who, from your point of view, are not people who should have power over you or your society?

____

____

____

____

____

____

____

____

____

____

____

____

____

____

____

Reason 7: Personal, party, and special or powerful group interests.

The elected representatives and the candidates do not only represent the people who voted for them, they also represent themselves and their party. It stands to reason that a representative balances their personal interests with the interests of the party and with the interests of the part of the electorate that voted for them. Furthermore, an elected official does not have to represent the part of the electorate that voted for them, to gain and maintain power it is sufficient for them to motivate the people to vote for them through fear or hatred of the opposition and, once in power, they can work for their personal goals and those of their party, not the interests of the people that voted for them.

Furthermore, it is very common for special interests or powerful groups, especially those with economic power, to influence politicians legally or illegally through campaign financing, lobbying, coercion, and corruption, so that representatives consider the interests of such groups above the interests of the people that voted for them.

When this happens, what is left is the government by those who represent themselves, their party, special interests, or powerful groups, and some interests of the people that voted for them, and who govern ignoring or against some of the interests of the citizens that voted for them and against, or ignoring, the interests of the population that did not vote for them.

In summary:

- Elected representatives also govern by taking into account their personal interests.

- The representatives usually belong to a political party that helped them gain power, so when they govern or legislate, they do so taking into account the interests of the political party, because they need it to stay in power.

- Elected representatives can be influenced by special interests or powerful groups that help or threaten them, so when they govern or legislate, they do so taking into account the interests of these groups.

- The representatives balance their personal interests, those of their political party, those of the special interest and powerful groups and those of their electorate when they make decisions. They may even disregard the interests of their electorate.

- This is not a democracy, it is the government of those who represent themselves, their political party, special interests, powerful groups, and some interests of the people that voted for them, and who govern against or ignore some interests of their electorate, and against or ignoring the interests of the population that did not vote for them.

Can you think of instances where elected officials have represented their political party and not you and other citizens? Do you know of cases in which your representatives have acted on behalf of some special interests and powerful groups and not on your behalf and that of other citizens? Do you think that when they work for their own objectives and interests, for those of their political party, or for those of the special interests or powerful groups, they are representing you?

____

____

____

____

____

____

____

____

____

____

Reason 8: Political parties that determine the options among which the citizen can choose.

The systems of electoral representation usually work with a political party system. Political parties are organizations with their own interests and ideologies that internally choose the candidates that they are going to present to citizens as options to represent them in public office.

In electoral representative democratic systems, even when independent candidates are admitted, it is highly advantageous for a candidate to be endorsed by a political party because the party assures them a certain amount of votes, financing, and the use of its political machinery to promote their candidacy. The first consequence of the political party system is that the decision of who is going to be the representative of the citizen is moved away from the citizen, since others, the members of the party, choose the candidates, and the citizen only chooses among the candidates presented by the parties. This means that the members of a political party decide the options from which citizens can choose. This gives the member of a party more power than that of the common citizen, since they are the ones who determine the options that the citizen will have. Under these circumstances, political parties function as powerful groups that generate an oligarchy and citizens can choose only among the options that the powerful groups present to them; this turns the election into a process where the citizen chooses among oligarchs.

In a political party system, the citizen is told: You can choose from among the options that we present to you. You can choose between the options that we choose for you.

In summary:

- Electoral representative democracy usually works with political parties. Party members often decide the candidates from which the citizens can choose, so citizens can only choose from options that others give them. This turns the electoral process to one of electing oligarchies.

Do you think that if others decide the options you can choose from you are really free? Have you found yourself in an election year and thought: "none of these candidates represents me"? Is power held by citizens if small groups (political parties) choose the options the citizens are going to have to choose from?

Reason 9: Inefficiency.

The electoral representative system often sacrifices the future for the present. Representatives, having a political career, are incentivized to generate short-term results. They are incentivized to carry out actions that attract the attention of the media and the public to quickly "solve" the problems they face; when sometimes real solutions require consistent long-term engagement and work. This turns the system of electoral representative democracy into an inefficient system. Representatives are incentivized to produce results, or what appear to be results, in the short term. They are not incentivized to undertake projects or strategies that require gradual and long-term solutions. As a result, many times the actions of governments only attack the symptoms of the problems they face and not their root causes.

The representatives are also incentivized to commit flashy actions that will attract attention without taking into account the consequences and repercussions that these actions will have in the long term.

Politicians are incentivized by the system to consider the effect of their actions on the popularity they have among their electorate, so when they are faced with a decision or a crisis, they have to ask themselves the following question:

How to solve the problem and get more popularity? Or, how to use the crisis to gain more popularity?

Being incentivized to decide according to these questions turns the decision-making process into one about gaining popularity, therefore, the decisions and actions of politicians are not necessarily those that can most efficiently solve problems, but rather the ones that can bring them the most popularity with the part of the electorate they need to gain or maintain power.

Furthermore, the divisiveness and polarization of the electorate means that when an opposition candidate is chosen, he has to work against the achievements of his predecessor. It is a system in which the work of an elected official can go against the work of the previous elected official without even looking for a midpoint, but seeking to generate a "clean slate". Since the actions of a representative or a party are oppressive for a sector of the population, when the opposition wins, in order to represent and work for the interests of those who they represent, they will have to undo and go against the work and achievements of the previous representative. This generates a highly inefficient system.

In summary:

- The representatives have to quickly demonstrate to their electorate that they are working for their interests, so they will opt for showy actions that appear to have fast results. This may mean attacking the symptoms and not the root of the problems their society faces.

- Representatives are incentivized to sacrifice long-term projects and results for short-term projects and solutions.

- Representatives can act without taking into account the long-term consequences of their actions.

- Representatives are encouraged to seek actions that make them more popular with the part of the constituency they need to stay in power and not the actions that best solve the problems they face.

- When a representative who was an opposition in the last electoral cycle wins, many times they need to eliminate laws or actions that the previous representative undertook.

Do you know of cases where politicians only attack the symptoms and not the root of the problems they face? Do you know of cases in which an elected politician tried to undo everything his predecessor did? Can you think of cases where a politician's short-term or flashy actions had negative long-term consequences for society? Do you think this is efficient?

Reason 10: If the winning representative is part of a legislative minority, they may not have the power to act or legislate in the interests of the people that elected them.

Most countries that are governed by the system of electoral representative democracy have a division of powers. In theory, the division of powers limits the powers of each elected official, be it a president, a governor, or a legislator. This is the difference between an absolute monarchy, a dictatorship, and electoral representative democracy. Usually, the representatives do not have absolute power, and being many and having a division of powers, they find themselves needing to negotiate among themselves to achieve their personal objectives, their political party's objectives, those of the special interests and powerful groups that helped them and perhaps, some of the objectives of their constituents. These negotiations, in which the elected official is forced to participate, limit their power, their opportunity to abuse power, and the amount of power they have to directly oppress the sectors of the population that did not vote for them. The limitation and separation of powers is necessary to avoid total oppression, but it is not enough to have a democracy. In fact, the separation of power might be similar to that of an aristocracy or a parliamentary monarchy, no one person holds absolute power, but the citizens do not rule themselves, they are ruled by the aristocrats, the ministers, and the royal family. The division of power is certainly a deterrent to the abuse of power by a single person, but it is not necessarily a deterrent for the abuse of the aristocracy or the oligarchy over the rest of the citizens.

On the other hand, if a representative is part of a minority in a legislative chamber, even if he has won in his local elections, he may not have actual power; therefore even if all, or the majority, of the members of a locality choose a representative, if he is part of the minority among elected representatives, he will not be able to do much for the interests of his constituents. All the interests of the members of a locality can be ignored if the majority of the other localities elect representatives of other parties or with other interests. So not only can the representative not represent the persons who voted for them, but even if they wanted, the representative may not have enough power to do one single thing in favor of those he represents. In this case, citizens are governed by the representatives of other localities or other sectors of the population that may have opposite views and interests. The division of powers can prevent total oppression, but it can also prevent members of some communities who think differently than most other communities in a society from the possibility of affecting or influencing their government's decisions.

In summary:

- The division of power will limit absolute power to reside in one person, therefore it will deter absolute oppression; but it will not eliminate the oppression of those without power by those with power.

- The division of powers may result in the representative of a locality having no power and being unable to legislate or act in favor of the interests of his constituents.

Has your representative ever won and then been unable to do anything because he is part of a minority? Did you feel represented in the government on that occasion? Do you think the way your country divides powers really protects you from oppression or from a group of representatives taking away your rights? Do you think that the division of powers in your country really makes the representatives work for you and not for their own interests, those of the special interest groups, and those of their political parties?

____

____

____

____

____

____

____

____

____

____

____

____

____

Reason II: Ruling representatives and governed electorate.

Electoral representative democracy separates citizens from government, from power, from the decision-making process, and from public affairs. That is, it separates the represented from the representatives, the electorate from the government, the citizens from the rulers; and it demands that the citizens only be active and participative during the elections. It disincentivizes any other form of public involvement and participation.

To be able to have a public official that governs there must be citizens who are governed, who are not involved in public affairs; the system requires a separation between ruler and ruled. In an electoral representative democracy, the citizen is asked to participate only to promote and vote for a representative and is kept from participating in anything else. The represented citizen is usually deprived of all real power, and his participation is in the best scenario relegated to criticizing, monitoring, and protesting. The electoral representative system removes the citizen from all positive action, from all action that implies collective work and social cohesion, from all effort that implies the development and construction of a society, and limits his participation to vote every certain number of years, and to complain. Electoral representative democracy is a system that discourages citizen participation, because if the citizen participates, the representative is no longer necessary.

Electoral representative democracy excludes the citizens from all public action, it keeps them from getting involved in the formation, the development, and creation of their society and their circumstances; it forces the citizen to accept and live in the world generated by the decisions and actions of his elected rulers. It is a system of social organization that sacrifices the individual, making him virtually powerless and excluding him from all important public action, reducing his freedom and power to a single act, that of voting to give power to a politician. The individual is powerless, cannot participate, and is of no importance. The only ones that have power and that matter are the politicians who manage to persuade the masses to vote for them.

Electing the person who governs and rules over you does not mean you live in a democracy, it just means that you elected the person who will have power over you. Some ancient civilizations elected their kings but that does not meant they lived in a democracy because the king had power over the citizens and governed over them. The citizens did not govern themselves, they were governed by the king they had chosen. Similarly, in the electoral representative democracy, the citizens do not govern themselves, they are governed by the oligarchy they chose.

This is the biggest argument that demonstrates the electoral representative system is not truly democratic. Democracy means government by the people, not government by the politicians elected by some of the people.

One of the biggest lies propagated worldwide through the last 200 years, is that voting to decide who holds power in the government is democratic. A democratic system enables, organizes, and permits the citizens to govern themselves. A system that permits the citizens to choose who will govern over them is not democratic; because citizens do not govern themselves, they are governed by the elected officials.

Would you consider yourself free and autonomous, if you could choose a person who would make all the decisions for you? Would you consider yourself free if you could choose a person that would decide what you should do with your life?

Electing government officials has nothing to do with democracy. In fact, some ancient civilizations elected their kings. Among them pre-democratic Athens, pre-republican Rome, and the medieval kingdoms of Poland, Ireland, Bohemia, among others 8. The free citizens or the noblemen of these kingdoms voted to elect their king. This was not considered a democracy, because once elected, the king ruled over the citizens, the citizens did not rule themselves. On some occasions, like that of pre-republican Rome, the kings were constricted by a constitution that, among other things, prohibited inheriting the throne. In other kingdoms, like the Polish- Lithuanian Commonwealth of the middle ages, the nobles could depose the king if they deemed him to be too oppressive. In other kingdoms, the nobles retained legislative power. These systems were called elective monarchies, not democracies, because the citizens did not govern themselves, they were ruled over by the king they elected. After the election, the king, or the king and the nobles had most of the political, fiscal, and military power in the society. An elective monarchy is not a system that permitted the citizens to govern themselves, it was a system that permitted the citizens to choose who would govern over them.

Furthermore, many of the countries that organize themselves with the electoral representative system give their presidents powers similar to those previously held by monarchs. Many presidents have the power to propose or veto legislation, they are the head of the government and the head of the state, they are the commanders of the armies, they can propose or veto fiscal policy and public spending, and are in charge of the judicial system. If a single person has all these powers, they are the rulers, even if it is for a limited amount of time. In many of our modern societies, the president is a temporary king in everything but name.

Other countries limit the power of the president or prime ministers, but the legislators or ministers function like an elective aristocracy or oligarchy. The power of the society is concentrated in the hands of the elected officials who rule over the citizens. They do not have absolute power, but, as a whole, they form a ruling class that governs the citizens for a limited amount of time.

Where the president has too much power, the system resembles an elective constitutional monarchy; where the power is distributed among the elected officials, the system is an elective constitutional oligarchy.

If the system does not permit the citizens to govern themselves, then the system is not democratic. If the citizen can elect who will govern over them but they can't govern themselves, then they do not live in a democracy.

Do you govern yourself or are you governed by the politician chosen by some of the citizens?

In summary:

- In order for a representative to exist there must be a group that is represented.

- In order for a representative to have power, the represented cannot have power.

- In order for someone to govern, someone else has to be governed.

- In order for the representative to act, whether legislating or executing, the represented has to be excluded from the actions of legislating or executing.

- If the citizen cannot participate, he does not live in a democracy.

- Electing who will have power to govern is not democratic.

- If the people do not have power, it is not a democracy.

- Government by those elected by some of the citizens is not government by the people.

- If a person, or a group of persons, govern and rule over all the citizens that means the citizens do not govern themselves. If the citizens do not govern themselves, they do not live in a democracy.

What do you think? Do you think that if citizens can only vote once every several years, and cannot get involved in other ways in the organization, decision-making processes, and the government of their society, the citizens still have power? Do you think that the citizens have the power to govern or that the representative has the power? In your country, who has more power, the representative or the citizens? How much citizen participation is there in your country? Does your government or your system stimulate or encourage citizen participation? What is citizen participation in your country?

____

____

____

____

____

____

____

____

____

____

____

____

Summary of Electoral Representative Democracy:

Electoral representative democracy is not a truly democratic system, because it is a system in which:

1. The representative is not elected by all citizens and therefore he does not represent all citizens, so the representative can ignore, work against the interests of, and oppress those who did not vote for him.

2. Candidates and political parties do not have to represent the people that voted for them, they just have to convince them that the opposing candidate is an enemy or bad for them.

3. Candidates and political parties polarize, divide, and destroy the social fabric by demonizing and condemning their opposition and those who vote for the opposition.

4. Representatives do not represent their electorate in everything. A representative can represent the people who voted for him on one issue and act against their interests on many other issues.

5. Representatives often balance their own interests with those of their political parties, the special interests and powerful groups that allow them to be in power, and those of the people who voted for them.

6. Representatives are limited human beings and one mistake will affect the entire society that they rule.

7. The Citizens are forced to choose between the options that the parties present to them. This means that the people in the

political parties have more power than those who are not part of the political parties.

8. Electoral representative democracy is a highly inefficient system because each elected government can work against the achievements of the previous administration.

9. Electoral representative democracy is highly inefficient because it incentivizes the rulers and representatives to work for flashy short-term results and to act seeking to gain popularity among their electorate and not to achieve the best results.

10. The separation of powers may render the representative of a locality unable to work for the interests and objectives of his constituents.

11. Once a government is elected some, or all, citizens lose their right to participate. In order for there to be representatives, the represented must be absent in the decision-making process. It is a system in which the representatives govern and have power and the represented are governed and have no, or little, power. Tis is the system in which the politicians elected by some of the citizens have power to rule over all the citizens.

Clearly, electoral representative democracy is not a system in which citizens govern themselves, it is not democratic or efficient. Therefore, if you want to be free, to participate in a free society, to choose, determine, or influence the circumstances in which you develop, live, and face, then you have to reject the electoral representative system. If you consider it unfair that a few people have most of the power in a society, that it is unfair and unacceptable that a few people can modify, influence, or determine the circumstances in which you live and the opportunities and freedoms you have, if you do not want to be oppressed, and you do not want to be an oppressor, it is time to look for a new system, to build a new society.

Societies did not start out being electoral representative democracies, they have changed and evolved. If you act, if you decide to be free, if you decide not to oppress and limit the freedoms, opportunities, and possibilities of other human beings, we can change the current system for a truly democratic one in which no one oppresses you; in which you are not afraid with every election that an inept person, a corrupt person, someone who will work against your interests, or an oppressor can win. We can change to a system in which you are part of the decision-making process and the construction of the world in which you live, of the circumstances that surround you and in which you develop. You have to decide if you will stay with the current system or if you will join the process of changing society and the system to a truly democratic one.

Decide, electoral representative democracy or freedom.

CHAPTER 3

Other forms of democracy

If electoral representative democracy is not real democracy, then what system is really democratic?

Almost all human beings on the planet were thought to believe that democracy means voting for representatives, but if that is not the case, then what system or process could really be democratic?

When I ask other people this question, I commonly receive the answer that all systems are corruptible, that in theory or on paper the systems might seem very good and perfect but once put into practice, the greed of human beings corrupts them. If you think this way, I ask you to stop for a moment and consider the following arguments.

You may be tired and disappointed in politics in general and in what "democratically" elected politicians have done to your country, and therefore by now you might be skeptical of democracy. But that is precisely my point, the system of electoral representative democracy was never democratic. You have not lived under a true democracy, neither in theory nor in practice. Think about your country's political problems, now compare them with the flaws that you can detect in the theory of the electoral representative system. The problem is not that electoral representative democracy has not been perfectly applied, the problem is that it is not really democratic. It is not a democratic system in theory and therefore it will never be a democratic system in practice. Therefore, what has failed us, is not democracy, but the systems that concentrate power in a few hands, the system in which the citizens decide who among them will have power to govern them.

Are you represented by your rulers?

____

Are you afraid that the elections will be won by a party or person who is going to go against your interests?

____

Do others decide what candidate options you will have?

____

You don't like any of the candidates and end up voting for the "lesser of two evils"?

____

Do you feel and think that those who vote for the opposition or the opposition candidates are stupid, ignorant, bad, oppressors, or enemies?

____

Do you think that politicians only work for their own interests and the interests of their political parties or special interests and powerful groups?

____

Do you feel that the state or the government imposes the laws on you?

____

Do you feel that you have no control or say over the world and the circumstances in which you live?

____

Do you feel that you are out of the political process?

____

Do you feel that politicians are only interested in you on election days?

____

Do you think you have the same power as all the other members of your society?

____

Do you think some members of your society have more power than others?

____

Do you think that those with more power influence or determine many of the circumstances in which you live?

____

Do you govern yourself, or are you governed by the politicians elected by some of the citizens?

____

These are not problems generated by democracy, they are problems generated by the electoral representative system, they are problems we can identify in its basic theory. Of course, corruption and greed magnify these problems; but these are problems and failures typical of the electoral representative system, not of democracy itself. Granted, it is difficult for systems to work as well in practice as they do in theory, but in the case of the electoral representative system, it is not only that the application can be improved, or that in practice it is not as good as it is in theory, but it is a system that generates oppression, polarization, social disintegration, concentration of power in a few hands, and is neither democratic nor efficient. If all systems are not as good in practice as in theory, we can at least look for a system that is better in theory than the current one.

If you give up right now, you are implicitly accepting that a few people should have the power to control and influence the society in which you live, your freedoms and responsibilities, your circumstances, opportunities, and possibilities; the impact that your society has on the environment, the impact that society has on your economy, on your health, on your psyche, on your time, and your life.

Can you think of other ways in which electoral representative democracy is not democratic, and limits and oppresses the freedoms and possibilities of the human being? Please take a moment to think about the particular electoral representative democracy system that your country is governed by. Are there certain mechanisms that lead you to conclude that the citizens do not govern themselves, or you are being oppressed.

Or can you think of a reason to stay in this system?

____

____

____

____

____

____

____

____

____

____

____

____

____

____

____

____

____

____

____

____

____

SECTION 2

How am I affected?

We have already concluded that electoral representative democracy is not democratic, but at this moment you may be wondering "But how am I affected by that? What does the political organization have to do with me? Why should I care about who is the ruler or legislator, who is president? How does "the system" affect me? How does the distribution of power affect me? You may think or have the idea that politics is not something that concerns you, involves you, affects you, or is worth being involved in. However, our social organization and the decisions made by the people with power affect almost every single aspect of our circumstances and, therefore, of our lives and, to some extent, who we are.

CHAPTER 1

What is politics?

Politics is the process by which decisions are taken that affect the members of a community or society. 2

It's that simple, the political process in your country is the process through which decisions are made that affect your life and that of all the other members of your society.

If a decision affects you, don't you think you should be involved in the decision-making process?

CHAPTER 2

What are the political systems?

Political systems are the systems, processes, organizations, and institutions that are used to take and execute the decisions that affect the members of a society.

In tyrannical systems, decisions are made by one or a few people who have the power to impose their decisions on the other members of society.

In democratic systems, decisions are made by all members of society and power is distributed equally among all members of society.

A system can be more or less tyrannical, and more or less democratic, depending on how much it involves all members of society in the decision-making process, who holds the power and how much power they have to impose decisions on the other members of the society.

The political system determines:

1) The persons who make decisions that affect all members of society.
   a) Who is involved in the decision-making process?
      i) Are all members of the society involved?
      ii) Are only a group of people involved?
      iii) Only one person makes all the decisions?

2) The type of participation that each person involved in the decision-making process has.
   a) It is not only important to know who makes the decisions but how much each person involved in the process matters or is decisive in this process.
   b) Does the participation of all members of society have the same importance, the same weight, and the same value?
   c) Does the participation of one person or group matter more than the participation of another person or another group?

3) The people or institutions that implement and execute the decisions that were taken.
   a) Who has the power to implement and execute the decisions?
   b) What kind of power and authority do these people have?
      i) Do they have economic power, police, political, or military power?
      ii) How much power do those who execute have over the other members of society?
      iii) Can they coerce people to obey through the threat of physical violence?
      iv) Can they execute actions through economic investments?
   c) What can they do with their power? How far can they exercise their power?
      i) Can they put a person in jail for disobeying? Can they hurt a person for disobeying? Can they take away a person's financial resources and belongings for disobeying? Can they kill a person for disobeying? Can they exclude a person from the decision-making process for disobeying?
      ii) What can the decision-makers and the people with power do?

4) To whom are the decision-makers and those who implement the decisions accountable to?
   a) Are the decision-makers and the people with power to implement and execute actions accountable to someone else?

b) Does someone have more authority than those who make decisions and those who execute them?
c) Who is this authority? Where does their authority derive from? And what powers do they have?
d) Who can hold those with power accountable?

Basically, the political structure determines who and to what degree is taken into account when making decisions; who will have power to execute and implement the decision, how much, what kind of power and over who they have the power; and to whom those who make the decisions and those who execute them will be accountable.

Now I ask you to analyze your situation for a moment. Are you part of the decision-making process of your society? How much are you taken into account? Are all members of society taken into account in the same way? Or, do some people have more power and are taken into account more than others? Who executes the decisions? How much power do they have over you? What happens when you disagree with a decision? Are you forced to do something you do not want to do? How can they compel or coerce you?

CHAPTER 3

How do political decisions affect you?

Whether you participate in the political process or not, the decisions taken inside the political system affect your personal development and your life. Political decisions affect you directly by demanding, prohibiting and guaranteeing you certain things; and indirectly by establishing the circumstances in which you develop and live.

Political decisions determine or influence:

1) The freedoms you do and do not have

2) The power you have over other members of society, and the power other members of society have over you.

3) The things you have to give to society:
    a) The taxes you have to pay.
    b) The freedoms you have to give up.
    c) The activities you have to participate in.
    d) The kind of power you can exercise or not over other members of society.
    e) The activities you can't do or will be regulated.

4) The things society is going to give you in return.
    a) The security you will have within society.
    b) The services that society will provide you.

> > i)   The infrastructure you will have access to.
> > ii) The public services you will have access to.
> > iii) Public education
> > iv) The social programs the society will implement.
> > > (1) Social Security.
> > > (2) Unemployment insurance
> > > (3) Public health programs
> > > (4) etc.
>
> c) The rights that society will give you.
> > i)   What are the personal rights that your society will protect.

5) The possibilities and opportunities that society will give or generate for you.

   a) Will society give you the opportunity to change your social or economic position or social class? or are positions and social classes determined by birth?

   b) Will society give you the opportunity and possibility to decide what to do with your own life? Will society require you to carry out certain activities? or will society only allow you to choose between certain options that someone else decided in advance?

6) The incentives and opportunities for citizen participation.

7) The incentives and opportunities to generate interaction among members of the society and social cohesion.

   a) How much and how do you interact with other members of society? From members of your society but with different social or economical status?

8) Incentives and opportunities for cultural development.

9) The impact that society and social activities will have on the environment and on people's health.

10) The way in which the political organization will be involved in the economy of the society and therefore of each and every one of

the members of the society.

How much do the 10 points mentioned above affect your life? What does your society require of you? What freedoms does your society limit? What kind of power does your society limit? What opportunities does it give you? What does your society give you and the other members of society? How much do you participate in the decision-making process to determine what freedoms you are going to have and what freedoms you are not going to have? How much do you participate in the decision-making process to determine what society is going to give to all its members?

____
____
____
____
____
____
____
____
____
____
____
____
____
____
____
____
____
____
____
____

CHAPTER 4

How does the economy affect you?

Economic circumstances are part of your social circumstances, of the way your society is organized. For human beings, the economy is one of the factors that most influences our development and our lives. Because economic circumstances determine how much time and effort a person has to dedicate to be able to meet their needs, generate enough resources to satisfy their desires, secure or improve their social position and / or the opportunities and possibilities that they have to undertake personal projects.

The economic circumstances of a society and its social structure determine:

1) The type of work that is available to each person; What skills, knowledge, physical and intellectual effort must be used for how many hours, and under what circumstances will the work have to be carried out to obtain:

2) The typeof economic remuneration that a person obtains for his work that allows him access to:

3) The type of products or services available to him; such as housing, food, education, health services, technology, entertainment, etc., available for consumption and use; which in turn allow him to have:

4) Socioeconomic position: the economic circumstances of an individual are not the only factor that determines their social position. However, they are the most important factor in a capitalist society. The quantity and type of products that a person owns, uses or consumes, the type of work he has to do, and the capital at his disposal, to a large extent determine the social position of human beings in the worldwide capitalist society in which we currently live.

5) Opportunities and possibilities to undertake personal projects. Human life may not only be working, commuting to and from work, training for work, resting and eating in order to continue working. Human beings can have personal projects such as having a family, making art, traveling, having close relationships with friends, opening their own business, building a house, raising animals, enjoying life, etc. Personal projects can be as varied as there are humans in the world. However, the economic circumstances may be adverse or reduce the possibilities for people to have time, energy and means for their personal projects, or the economic circumstances might increase the possibilities and opportunities people have to engage on their own personal projects.

   a) If the economic circumstances require that all human beings dedicate 10 or 12 hours of their day to work, then the time they will have for their personal projects will be very limited.

   b) If economic circumstances make it impossible for a lower or lower middle class person to open a business or travel, then personal projects are completely affected or blocked by their economic circumstances.

For example: It is very clear how the economic circumstances affect people in every level of their lives when the economic circumstances only permits a group or class of people the options to work for subsistence in polluting mines or factories, and the workers end their labor days tired and sick, and therefore cannot enjoy their family, friends or undertake other personal projects, and they also die relatively young, because they are poisoned by polluting gases from the factories.

Now reflect a little on your own life. How many opportunities do you have because you were born in your society and in your socioeconomic position? Would your opportunities have been different if the economy had been different? How much time do you spend or the people around you devote to work, and all activities related to work? Have you changed your socioeconomic level during your life? Have you been able to rise or fall considerably in socioeconomic status thanks to your work and effort? How many people do you know who have changed their socioeconomic status? How many personal projects do you have that are not work related? How much time do you have for your personal projects? How much control do you have on the economy of your country and the opportunities available to you and everyone else?

CHAPTER 5

The economy and the environment

The economy not only determines the time and effort you have to dedicate to work, the remuneration you can obtain, what you can do with this remuneration and your social position thanks to your economic position; The economy and the economic system also determine the impact of production, consumption and waste on the environment and on your health.

The economic system and economy determine:

1. The products that are being and will be produced.

2. The natural, human, and technological resources that production requires.

3. The environmental impact generated by the extraction of natural resources needed for production.

4. The environmental impact generated by the transformation of natural resources into a product.

5. The useful life of a product.

6. The environmental impact that the product will have during its useful life.

7. The environmental impact that the product will have once it is considered trash or waste.

8. The impact on human health when the product is produced.

9. The impact on human health when the product is consumed.

10. The impact on human health when the product becomes trash or waste.

CHAPTER 6

Politics and the economy

The governments of countries around the world stimulate and regulate the economy through laws, regulations, subsidies, taxes, trade agreements, tariffs, public spending, the amount of money printed and how they introduce it to the economy, control of some sectors of the economy, public services and infrastructure, the definition of private property, etc.

The political process influences the economy of society and your economy by deciding:

1) To whom and what amount of taxes will be charged and collected.

2) If the government will ask for loans and accumulate debt?

3) What is the government's money going to be spent on?

4) What economic or financial actions are not going to be allowed and how are they going to be regulated.

5) Will the possession of money be allowed to generate power, be it economic, political, or military power?

6) Will the impact of the economic activity on the environment be regulated?

7) Is the impact of the economic activity on the health of the members of society going to be regulated?

8) Is the power employers have over workers regulated?

9) What rights will workers have?
   a) Maximum working hours?
   b) Minimum wage?
   c) Safety at work?
   d) Holidays?
   e) How many days a week people need to work?
   f) Is there any protection against unfair dismissal and discrimination, etc.?

10) How much economic inequality will the government allow? Is it going to promote equality?

11) How will the government protect the economy of the members of the society?

12) Are there going to be trade agreements with other countries? And to what purpose?

13) If it is going to promote foreign investment, how and on which sectors of the economy and population?

14) In what economic activities and decisions will the society as a whole be involved?

15) What actions will the national bank take?
   a) Will it print more money or withdraw money from circulation?
   b) Will it give loans and with what interest rates to citizens, corporations, banks, or groups?
   c) Will it introduce the new money through public spending or through the financial system?

16) What is considered private property and what are the rights and responsibilities of the property holders?

These are some of the economic decisions in which governments are involved.

Through the social organization system, political decisions are made that affect the economy. These decisions influence every aspect of the economy including the job options available to you, the time you have to spend at work, the products you can buy, and the impact that your society and its economy will have on the environment. If you live in a democratic system, in theory, you are part of the decision-making process that determines everything from your freedoms, your opportunities, your power, your economy, and your environment. If you live in a tyrannical system, others make the decisions and you live in the world and the circumstances generated by their decisions.

Are you part of the decision-making process that determines or influences the economy? The jobs available? Are you part of the decision-making process that determines where the government will invest public funds? Do you participate in the decision-making process to determine workers' rights? Can you influence how much power those with the most money have in society? Do you have any say concerning the impact that the economic activity will have on the environment or peoples' health? Are you involved in the decision-making process that determines or influences the economic activity that has such a great impact on your life?

____

____

____

____

____

____

____

____

____

____

____

CHAPTER 7

Politics and your circumstances

Through its control or influence on the economy, security, education, the environment, food, health, social cohesion, and all the other aspects previously mentioned, the political system in which you live, and the decisions that are made and executed through it, determine or influence almost all the circumstances in which you have lived, developed, and faced during your life.

Your circumstances affect you in the following ways:

1. Your development is affected by your circumstances.

2. Your life, freedoms, opportunities, and possibilities are affected or determined by your circumstances.

How is my development related to my circumstances?

You are a human being and like every human you are a living being made up of the elements Oxygen, Carbon, Hydrogen, Calcium, Phosphorus, Potassium, Sulfide, Sodium, Chlorine, and Magnesium. These 11 elements come together in different ways to generate the human body. The DNA of each human has the information that organizes these 11 elements to form each body part of each human being.

Every human being's DNA contains enough similarities for each human being to be considered human, but enough variations for each human being to be considered an individual. All human beings share at least 99.9% of their DNA and have a maximum of 0.1% of their genes organized in a unique way.

This 99.9% similarity between human beings is what gives us human qualities, our skin, height range, hands, feet, internal organs, muscles, and even brains. Part of the remaining 0.1% determines certain differences between our human qualities such as the color of skin, hair, eyes, and certain specific traits for each individual. However, the similarity in DNA that we humans share does not mean that we are all 99.9% similar. The differences between each of us increases because not all genes are "expressed" in the same way. This means that a human being can share a gene with another human being, but in one person, the gene is expressed in one way and in the other person the gene is expressed differently. Genes contain a wide range of information that allows a certain range of possibilities and within the possibilities of each gene, a single possibility is "expressed" in every human. The expression of the gene is called epigenetic and depends on two factors:

1) Hereditary information passed down by the mother:

The ovum has information on how to interpret the DNA provided by the mother and the father to the offspring. This means that the mother passes on information to her offspring about which genes are to be expressed in what way. The mother not only gives part of her DNA, she also gives part of the code that determines how the DNA will be interpreted to develop the offspring's body. This information on how to interpret DNA is a combination of what she received from her own mother and the mother's personal development in her own circumstances.

The effects of the circumstances on who you are start here. The circumstances in which your mother lived influenced the epigenetic code that she passed down to you interprets your DNA; and therefore, the circumstances in which your mother lived determine certain characteristics that you have: it can be your height, your tendency to accumulate fats, your ability to concentrate or have abstract thought, your violent tendencies, etc.

2) The circumstances:

At each stage of his life, the human being develops, lives, and faces his circumstances. Each individual's DNA develops the body according to its circumstances. This means that in the DNA of each individual there is a range of options that can be developed, and it is the interpretation that the organism makes of its circumstances that determines what DNA information is used to develop the body of the individual. The way genes are expressed in the development of the individual is, in part, determined by the individual's interpretation of its circumstances. Two exactly identical genes in different circumstances can be expressed differently. The circumstances, especially of the fetus and during early childhood, determine which part of the DNA is going to be expressed.[3]

For example, the DNA of a human being has the information that determines his height range, but his specific height will depend on the nutrients the fetus receives, the food and nourishment the baby and child receives, the exercise and the fiscal space in which he lives the first years of his life. The same genetic information regarding height but completely different circumstances can result in people with very different heights.

The DNA of a human being might contain the potential to be a great athlete, but it depends on the food and training if this potential as a great athlete is going to develop or if his body will be weak, obese, or flabby.

In the DNA of an individual there may be the potential to develop a brain with very high capacities for abstraction and rationalization, but it will be the combination of the code passed by the mother, food during pregnancy, childhood, adolescence and youth, and the use that the individual makes of his brain, which will determine the abstraction capacities of the developed brain.

The circumstances in which you are gestated and born, in which you develop, live, and face, especially the first years of your life, determine and influence what part of your DNA is going to be expressed. This means that your circumstances have influenced and determined some of your physical, intellectual, and psychological qualities. You are who you are, in part, due to your circumstances.

If the circumstances in which each human being develops would only determine their height, complexion, weight, the health of their skin, hair, and internal organs, then the circumstances could be of limited consequence and importance for the development of each individual and each society. However, the circumstances also influence intellectual capacity, social or antisocial, violent or empathic tendencies, sexual development, and the psychological health and state of mind of every human being. This means circumstances are as important as DNA in the process of developing the human being.

For example: If an experiment was carried out in which a person is cloned three times and one of the clones was given very healthy, balanced nutrition full of vitamins and minerals. Another is given enough junk food to fill the stomach, and the last one is constantly deprived of food and is subjected to famine and malnutrition, all three clones, even when they contain the same genetic information, will develop a different body and brain; There would be great similarities between the three, but the change in diet would cause the development of the three to be uneven.

If a similar experiment was carried out and the three clones were given the same nutritious diet, but one of them grows and develops in a home and an environment without affection and full of violence; another develops in an environment full of love, acceptance, and intellectual education; and the last one grows up in an environment without violence but without affection, attention, or education, we can assume that the intellectual and emotional qualities that each individual will develop will be different.

This does not mean that the human being is 100% determined by his circumstances, but that circumstances play a fundamental role in the development of every human being.

You are who you are, in part due to the circumstances in which you developed, and the circumstances in which you developed were determined or influenced by the social, political, and economic system and the decisions made and executed by the people with power in this system.

The circumstances in which you developed depend on the social, political, and economic system and the decisions that are made and executed within this system. You are who you are, in part, due to this system. The decisions being made at this moment inside the system will determine or influence the circumstances in which all babies, children, youth, and adults will develop from now on. These circumstances will affect not only what they can and cannot do, their opportunities and freedoms, but how and who they will be.

Taking into account the way in which circumstances have affected your personal development, do you think that the decisions that affect and influence the circumstances in which you and all the members of your society and all the generations to come will live and develop should be in the hands of a few politicians? Do you think that a few people should be in control of the circumstances that affect you and all other human beings so much?

____

____

____

____

____

____

____

____

____

What is the relationship between the circumstances, the political system, the individual freedoms, and the opportunities and possibilities every human being has?

Social circumstances not only determine or influence all the circumstances in which you develop physically, intellectually, and psychologically, but they are also the circumstances in which you will live, which you will confront, and in which you will act during your life. First and foremost, your circumstances are part of the reason why you are who you are, and your circumstances will limit or potentiate your opportunities and your freedom to act with respect to what you want to do or what projects you would like to have.

Due to the circumstances in which you developed, you are who you are today; and due to the circumstances you face today and the decisions you make today, you will be who you will be tomorrow. As you continue to develop, part of your development in the future depends on who you are now as a result of your past and the decisions you make when facing the current circumstances in which you live. What you can or cannot do, the opportunities that you will have and those that you will not have, the opportunities and possibilities you have to engage in personal projects, if you will be oppressed, exploited, or used, if you will have the option to oppress and exploit others, if you are going to have time to socialize, to dedicate yourself to learning, to art, to establish close relationships, or if all your time will be spent working and procuring commodities, or if you will have to be afraid of the people around you. All of this depends on the circumstances in which you live and these circumstances depend on the social, political, and economic organization of your society.

Who you are today is a consequence of your DNA, your decisions, and your past circumstances, which were the consequence of political and economic systems and decisions. Who you will be tomorrow depends on the circumstances that allow you to have certain options, possibilities, and freedoms. You will only be able to choose between the options provided by your circumstances, and you will only be able to use your will and your freedom within what your circumstances allow, and these circumstances that you have today and that you will have tomorrow, are the result of the political and economic systems, and decisions taken and executed through them.

This might seem obvious, but the repercussions are immense.

Let's do a little exercise to reflect on how circumstances affect you right now.

Think about the food you like and that you know is nutritious and healthy for you:

____

____

____

Think about what you would like to do with your time if you had the opportunity and freedom to do it:

____

____

Think about where you would like to go to have a good time:

____

Think about your plans for the next 5, 10, and 20 years, what would you like to do with your life during this time?

____
____
____
____
____
____
____
____

These things, so simple and obvious, are completely related to your circumstances. What you're going to make of your life, what you can achieve, partly depends on you, on your effort and your abilities, but also on your circumstances. The opportunities and possibilities you have to achieve what you want to do depend on your circumstances, what type of society you live in, your socioeconomic position within this society and what opportunities this society gives you.

Now think if you had all the money in the world, if you were the son of a millionaire or a king:

What would you eat?

____
____

What could you do with your free time?

____
____
____
____

Where would you go to have a good time?

____

Think about the plans you could have in 5, 10, and 20 years. What would you like to do with your life during this time?

____
____
____

———————————————————

———————————————————

———————————————————

———————————————————

———————————————————

Now think, if you were in a third world country with a bad economic crisis, you have a mother that works but earns little because it is a patriarchal society and your father had an accident at work so he cannot move or work. Now think:

What food could you eat under those circumstances?

———————————————————

———————————————————

———————————————————

How much free time would you have? Or what would you spend all your time on?

———————————————————

———————————————————

Where could you go to have a good time?

———————————————————

What kind of plans could you have for the next 5, 10, and 20 years? What could you do with your life during this time?

———————————————————

———————————————————

———————————————————

———————————————————

———————————————————

The possibilities, the options you have in your life, depend on the circumstances in which you live.

Do you want to start a family? Think about what that would be like if you lived in a monarchy where the king has the right to sleep with the bride on your wedding night. Think about what it would be like to start a family if you lived in a neighborhood full of violence, where death and rape are an everyday occurrence. Think about what it would be like to start a family if the price of education, housing rents, health insurance, and nutritious food increase and go up and up, while wages do not go up, or rather, they go down and you have to spend 10 or 12 hours a day at work.

Your circumstances not only affect you in an abstract way in your physical and psychological development, they affect every moment of your daily life. It is not only possible to aspire to different things if you live in different circumstances, but even if you aspire to something as general as having a family of your own, the options in front of you, the possibilities of what you can or cannot do, will be completely different according to your social circumstances.

Now think about your life plan or a project in your life:

____
____
____
____
____
____
____
____
____
____
____

Could you achieve that life plan or that project in other circumstances?

____

Would you even have that life plan or project if you were in other circumstances?

____

Are there other political or economic circumstances that would allow you to carry out this life plan more easily? Are there other political and economic circumstances that would make it impossible for you to carry out your life plan? Could you aspire to "a better life plan" in other political and economic circumstances?

____

____

____

____

____

____

____

____

____

____

All the circumstances in which you develop, in which you live, and which you face, are affected or determined by the system of social organization in which you live and by the people with power in this system.

Who took the decisions that determined the circumstances in which you have developed so far? Who will make decisions today that will determine the circumstances affecting your future development and determine what opportunities, possibilities, and freedoms you are going to have in the future? Who makes the decisions that determine the circumstances that influence you so much? Are you part of the decision-making process?

____

____

____

____

____

____

____

____

____

____

____

____

____

____

____

____

____

In summary

The way your society is organized determines who has the power to make and execute the decisions that will affect all your circumstances. These circumstances affect your development and they affect how and who you are. These circumstances will also determine what opportunities, possibilities, and freedoms you have now and will have in the future; therefore they influence who you are and what you can do with your life.

Right now, you have the potential to decide if you are going to continue allowing others to make and execute all the political and economic decisions that determine your circumstances that influence you so much; or if you are going to change the system to be able to be part of the decision-making process and the execution of these decisions that determine the circumstances you want to have, to have the options and possibilities you want to have, to be able to freely choose your life plan, and be able to carry it out.

CHAPTER 8

Why form and be part of a Society?

The human being is a social being by nature. This not only mean that human beings seek to be close to each other or to interact. Rather, by establishing social relationships, human beings seek to form common projects. Forming projects together is one of the activities that has helped humans develop beyond beings living in caves. The capacity for abstraction of human beings, their intellectual capacities, their freedom, and their ability to collaborate, allows human beings to develop projects they share in common that would have been impossible for a single human to achieve. This ability to develop joint projects led the human being to go from caves to towns, from being hunter gatherers to developing agricultural societies, to the industrial revolution, to developing economies, cities, nations, etc. This ability to develop complex common projects gives us the ability to stop being completely in the hands of external circumstances. Without the ability to collaborate and work together, we would be 100% at the mercy of the circumstances. This ability to socialize and work together gives us the opportunity to influence or control our circumstances.

The union of two people to develop a project together can lead to the elaboration of more complex projects than those that can be developed and carried out by a single person. Therefore, establishing a partnership with another person opens many possibilities for the human being.

Each person who joins a society brings forth and contributes a wide range of extra possibilities that are open to all others in the society. Each new human being in a society brings with him knowledge, subjective points of view, physical and intellectual capacities, time, energy, and effort, and a free inner world that can contribute to the society as a whole, to particular projects and to the implementation of said project.

For example: A human will hardly be able build a house alone. A society of many humans, in collaboration, can build tall buildings, dams, etc.

A person alone can hardly develop the medicines that have saved so many lives; or the technology that has opened up so many possibilities to humanity.

Think about what your life would be like if you did not have contact with any other human beings and you did not have access to any of the benefits that the collaboration of all human beings who have gone before you has developed. You would have no language, you would not have art, you would not have technology, you would have no family, no friends, you would not read novels or watch movies and series, you would know nothing about cooking, you would not know what you can eat and what would kill you, you would not know about food techniques, hunting, or agriculture, you would not know medicine, etc. Can you think of your life like this? Would it be desirable to live such a life? Not a life in which, with all the knowledge you have of the natural world and with technology and tools developed by other human beings, you go to a cabin to live as a hermit, because that is a life in which you make use of knowledge and technology developed before you thanks to human collaboration. But a life in which there has never been human collaboration, in which you have always been isolated from every human being. Think about the things you want and what you enjoy and love in life. How many of these things are possible thanks to the interaction and collaboration among human beings?

____

____

____

CHAPTER 9

Freedom and Society

All the advantages that can be achieved thanks to cooperation among people do not remove the fact that in order to cooperate there must be certain organization that determines the rules of coexistence and certain things that individuals have to do or from which they have to restrain from doing, in order to belong to a society. What each member of society has to do or cannot do to be part of a society, and what each member of society will gain by being part of the society, is part of what determines the social and political system in which he lives.

The society is not free, it is a tyrannical society when:

- The members of the society are coerced into belonging to the society.

- A social system is imposed on the members of the society.

- In this social system, others have the power to make all decisions that affect all members of the society, and the circumstances in which they all live and develop.

- In this system, some have the power to coerce others to act in certain ways, not to act in other ways, or to establish limited options from which the person can choose.

- In this social system, which was imposed on the person, others, those with power, decide what advantages, benefits, rights, opportunities, possibilities, and freedoms will be available to the members of society.

A free society is one in which:

- The members of the society freely decide to be members or not of the society.

- Members of the society can choose or modify the system by which the society is organized.

- In the chosen social system, all members of society can participate and are taken into account equally in the decision-making processes that will affect the life and circumstances of all who live in the society.

- Through this decision-making process in which they freely participate, members of society decide what they will prohibit, what they will restrain from doing and give up, or what they are willing to do to belong to the society.

- Through this decision-making process in which they freely participate, members of the society also decide what benefits and rights all members of society will have; projects they want to do together, and what circumstances they will seek to develop through their joint actions and projects.

    ○ This means that the members of the society decide freely not to do some things and to do some other things, to be able to generate the circumstances, possibilities, opportunities, and freedoms that are only possible through collaboration with other members of the society.

Free human beings, by developing a free society, decide to limit certain personal freedoms, but in doing so they potentiate and generate other freedoms and expand their options and possibilities.

The formation of free societies, that develop and decide their joint projects, the future they strive to achieve, and that freely develop plans to achieve such futures and put them into action, acting and striving for the goals and future they decided upon, is one of the most gratifying activities for humans, and one of the activities that most potentiates the possibilities, options, and freedoms of the human being.

How free is your society? How involved are you in the decision-making process of your society? How much freedom do you have to choose to belong or not to your society? Can you decide the benefits you get for belonging to your society? Can you decide the circumstances that will be created thanks to the collaboration of the members of your society?

CHAPTER 10

Individual vs. Social Freedom

In a free society, social freedom implies restriction of the freedom of action of each individual according to what is freely agreed upon by all members of society. This means that if alone or outside of society, the individual can perform certain actions, or that if in a non-free society the individual can use his power to perform certain actions. In a free society, the power of the individual is necessarily restricted so that it is not oppressive to the other members of society, and the freedom of action of the individual is limited according to what is freely agreed upon by all members of society. This implies that in order to belong to a free society, the human being, voluntarily and freely, decides to act in a certain way and not to act in certain other manners. Because it was a free and voluntary decision of the person to belong to the society and accept what actions will be permitted, which ones prohibited, and which required to be able to be part of the society, then social freedom does not really limit individual freedom. Rather, it is a free, voluntary, and premeditated decision and commitment of one's own, to perform certain actions and not perform certain other actions.

Society is oppressive to the freedom of the human being when he is not part of the decision-making process that determines what every member of the society can and cannot do, and what he is required to do to be able to belong to the society, and what he will get in return. If society is free, the individual retains his freedom of action even if there are certain actions that he decides not to do in order to belong to the society, since not doing some actions was his decision in the first place; but if society is not free, each restriction that society makes on individual liberties is an oppression of the freedom of each individual.

To understand these distinctions in a simple way, we can imagine a person who voluntarily decides to get on a plane. When deciding to get on the plane, you decide the destination and you are aware that you will have to be inside the concealed space of the plane for a certain amount of time and that after that time you will arrive at your desired destination. Your person's physical freedom is restricted on the plane, since you have to remain in your seat and cannot leave the plane for a time, but this restriction is not an oppression. This restriction is a consequence of your decisions; you decided to restrict your freedom of movement for a couple of hours to achieve the goal of reaching your destination. Conversely, if you are kidnapped and put on a plane for the same amount of hours and arrive at the same destination, you are being oppressed, your freedom of action and movement is being taken away from you.

In a free society, the members freely decide to limit certain freedoms to achieve certain common objectives and to potentiate other freedoms. In an oppressive society, others decide to limit everyone's freedoms to achieve the objectives decided by the oppressors.

How free are you in your society? What do you have to do to belong to your society? What is prohibited to you because you belong to your society? Is what you are prohibited from doing a limitation to your freedom? Are you coerced to do or not do something? Is what you have an obligation to do an oppression of your freedom? Who decides what you can or cannot do and what you have to do in order to be part of your society? Did you decide freely or did others decide and force you to obey?

____

____

____

____

____

____

____

____

CHAPTER II

Collaboration vs. Oppression

The human's freedom of action is the possibility to decide what to do with one's own time, energy, body, and intellectual capacity. The freedom of the human being expands and potentiates or limits and contracts according to the circumstances in which he finds himself. If humans live completely alone and do not form societies, then the possibilities and options that humans will have will be very limited and they will be free to act within the limited options that their solitude allows them.

If the human being decides to develop societies to collaborate with other human beings, he can generate circumstances and projects that allow him to expand his opportunities and possibilities beyond what he can access and achieve alone. This means that by uniting one's own efforts, time, and capacities with those of other people, many more options open up from which each person can choose. It is very important to be aware that one of the options that opens up for humans when they develop societies is to oppress and use other people as tools and objects. When one person oppresses another, he usually does so to increase his possibilities and opportunities at the expense of the other person's freedom and opportunities. This means that the oppressor uses the time, intelligence, body, energy, and effort of the oppressed to increase his own opportunities, possibilities, and freedoms while reducing those of the oppressed. If a human being expands his opportunities, possibilities, and freedoms by reducing the opportunities, possibilities, and freedoms of another human being, then he is oppressing. If two humans decide to collaborate freely and with the combination of their time, effort, intelligence, body, and energy they create opportunities for both of them that would be impossible without their collaboration, then both persons increase their freedoms, opportunities, and possibilities. A free society is one in which two or more people freely come together to collaborate and increase the opportunities, possibilities, and freedoms for every member of that society.

However, coexistence and the formation of societies does not increase all freedoms in an absolute manner; it also restricts other options and freedoms. To develop a free society, the members of the society must decide on their own what freedoms they are going to limit, what freedoms they are going to renounce, what activities and actions they commit to carry out in order to be part of the society and obtain the freedoms, opportunities, possibilities, and circumstances they have decided they want to generate through their collaboration. It is very important that we pay special attention to the freedoms, possibilities, and opportunities people renounce, and the actions they commit to do in order to be part of the society; because in a free society many of the freedoms that human beings have to give up in order to be part of a free society, are freedoms to use their power to take away the freedoms of others.

In a free society the people freely decide:

1. The circumstances, opportunities, possibilities, and freedoms that they wish to obtain through their collaboration and the formation of their society.

2. The freedoms, options, opportunities, and possibilities that they had before joining the society and that they limit or renounce in order to be part of their society.

3. The freedoms, opportunities, and possibilities that arise due to the formation of the society, but that the people themselves freely decide they are going to restrict, limit, or renounce, in order to be able to develop the society they wish to have, and to generate the circumstances, freedoms, possibilities, and

opportunities they decided they wanted to strive for.

4. To restrict or eliminate the use of power that a human being has over other human beings in order to protect the freedoms of all members of society.

5. To carry out certain actions so that in collaboration with the other members of the society they can generate the society, circumstances, opportunities, and possibilities that they decided they wish to obtain through their social collaboration.

We will now develop these ideas further:

1. In a free society, the people freely decide the circumstances, opportunities, possibilities, and freedoms that they wish to obtain through the collaboration and formation of their society.

Collaboration between human beings generates circumstances that open up certain possibilities and opportunities that are beyond the reach of the human being who lives or acts alone. However, it is impossible to generate an infinite amount of possibilities, opportunities, possibilities, and circumstances through the development of a society; the social structure and actions of individuals within the society generate the circumstances that determine which opportunities and possibilities will be available to the members of the society and which will not. To have a free society, the members of the society have to decide what circumstances they want to generate in order to obtain the opportunities, possibilities, and freedoms they wish to obtain; recognizing that they cannot obtain an infinite number of freedoms and opportunities, and that the choice to open a possibility, to receive a benefit, may imply not receiving another benefit and rejecting other opportunities. In a free society, human beings freely decide what they want to obtain from their society, from their collaborative efforts, from their rejection of some other opportunities, possibilities, and freedoms.

For example, a person living alone, without society, would have to build their own house, make their own clothes to ward off the cold, make their own hunting tools, grow their own food, fend off predators alone, and cannot enjoy the company of other human beings, of coexistence, of art, of literature, of entertainment, of culture. Alone the human would not be able to experience the emotions that arise through coexistence, emotions like love, affection, attraction to other people, joint purpose with other people when undertaking a collaborative project; to enjoy the fruit of the labour and knowledge of other humans, to enjoy sex and all other activities that are only possible when two or more human beings interact.

A person can decide that they want to live in a society so that, through collaboration with other human beings, they can ensure their safety against predators, facilitate their access to food, improve their home, enjoy the company of other human beings, etc.

2.   In a free society, the people freely decide the freedoms, options, opportunities, and possibilities that they had before joining the society and that they limit, or renounce, in order to be part of their society.

Human beings alone, without society, may have certain freedoms that are restricted when they are part of a society. In a free society, the human being freely decides which of his freedoms that he had before joining the society he is going to restrict or renounce in order to be part of the society.

For example: If a human being who did not live in society has the freedom to defecate anywhere, when forming a society, the other members of the society can ask or demand that he defecate only in designated places.

The freedoms, opportunities, and possibilities that humans enjoy alone, without interaction or socialization with other humans, are in fact very basic, therefore, when the human decides to restrict or reject some of those opportunities, possibilities, and freedoms, he is renouncing very basic freedoms, opportunities, and possibilities and will gain wider, more complex opportunities, possibilities, and freedoms which he himself decided to strive for.

3. In a free society, the people freely decide the freedoms, opportunities, and possibilities that arise due to the formation of the society, but the people themselves freely decide what they are going to restrict, limit, or renounce, in order to be able to develop the society they wish to have, and to generate the circumstances, freedoms, possibilities, and opportunities they decided they wanted to strive for.

When a human being unites his efforts, intelligence, time, and talent to that of other human beings, his possibilities, opportunities, and freedoms multiply, and suddenly there are options before him that did not exist before; however, in order to form a free society and achieve the goals of all members of society, members of society may ask their members not to make use of certain options, freedoms, and possibilities.

For example: Thanks to the fact that human beings collaborate in society, they have the possibility of producing products in industrial quantities, but to do so they have to use many natural resources. The human being has the possibility of producing in industrial quantities because he lives in a society, the possibility of industrial production is a direct result of the human being living in society. If the members of the society decide to limit the exploitation of natural resources, the capacity for industrial production is limited, but since industrial production is a result of social collaboration, then the only thing that is being limited is a possibility and opportunity that was generated through the formation and development of the society. The existence of the society generates a possibility, which is then limited by the members of the society. Although this opportunity is limited by society, the opportunity itself only exists thanks to the society, so in reality the human being continues to gain more from participating in the society than from not participating. What is being limited was only an option that existed due to the formation of the society.

If the human being without society has the possibility of doing only ten things, and the human being in society gains the opportunity and possibility of doing twenty things, but the other members of society ask him not to do five things in order to generate the circumstances they all strive for, then the person in such a society will have fifteen opportunities. Alone the person has ten opportunities, in the society without limitations, he has twenty opportunities, in the society with limitations and restrictions he has fifteen opportunities, so even with the limitations, the person gains opportunities and possibilities through the formation of the society.

The process by which members of the society determine what freedoms, opportunities, and possibilities everyone is going to renounce, determines how free and democratic a society is.

4. In a free society, the people freely decide to restrict or eliminate the use of power that a human being has over other human beings in order to protect the freedoms of all members of society.

When forming societies, power relations are generated. That is, differences are generated between the characteristics or circumstances of each individual that give some the power and possibility of inflicting harm on others, or coercing them to act or not act according to what they want, or to determine the circumstances in which everyone is going to live. In a free society, members freely choose which power relations they will allow and how much power and its use they will allow.

For example: to be part of a society, a man is asked not to force a woman to have sex. If the man lives alone without society, he would not even have the possibility of sex. If the human being is completely alone and is not part of a society, there is no chance or opportunity for him to have sex. Since the human being is in society, there is a possibility that he will have sexual relations. If the man coerces or forces a woman to have sex, he is using his power to satisfy his desire while oppressing and taking away the freedom of the woman to do with her time, her body, her effort, her energy, her life, and sexuality that which she decides to do. Due to the fact that the man lives in society, he has the possibility of having consensual sexual relations with a woman who freely decides to dedicate a certain amount of her time, energy, and life to sexual activity with him. But this possibility that is generated thanks to the formation of society does not mean that there is an obligation. The possibility for people to have sexual relations is only available when there is human interaction and society; if the society is free, no one can coerce someone else to have sex; if the society is free, sexual relations only occur between people who freely decide to have sexual relations; if one person forces or coerces another to have sexual relations, he is taking away the freedom of the coerced party, thus destroying the free society. If, as a condition of belonging to society, all people are asked to only have consensual sexual relations where two people freely decide to have sex, they are not taking away a freedom, but their power to oppress is being limited. If the man is alone, he does not have the possibility of having sex, if he is in society, he has the possibility of having it, if he is required to only have sex while respecting the freedom of the other person, the man continues to have more options and possibilities than if he was not in the society. Therefore, society is not limiting or oppressing him, but is giving an opportunity and possibility, as long as he respects the freedom of the other person. If a man uses his physical, economic, or political strength to coerce or force a woman to have sex with him, then he is not using his freedom but using his power over her. The restriction of power is the restriction of an opportunity to oppress generated due to the formation of the society, but it is not the restriction of a freedom.

If a human being without society has only one possibility available to him, and through being in a society he gains the possibility of doing twenty more thing, but of those, five involve taking away the freedom of other people through the use of power, then the other people, by joining the society, obtain new freedoms, possibilities, and opportunities, but also the possibilities of being oppressed. That is, a person without society can only do one thing, but he is not oppressed by anyone. If this person enters a society that allows him to do ten more things, but that generates circumstances in which he can be oppressed in another five different ways, then the person obtains ten new opportunities for freedom and five opportunities for oppression. In this society, there would be one person who obtains fifteen new opportunities to increase his freedom without oppressing the others, and five opportunities to increase his freedom by oppressing the others; while the other persons obtain ten new opportunities without oppressing the other and five possibilities of being oppressed by the first person. The first person is obtaining more opportunities than the second one, therefore there is a disproportionality in the benefits that the members of the society obtain; furthermore, one obtains more benefits due to the power he has to oppress the other member of the society, not thanks to the free collaboration of both people. If, in order to form a free society, both people reach an agreement in which they determine that they cannot oppress the other members of the society, then the second person loses the possibility of being oppressed, and the first person loses the five possibilities to gain opportunities through oppression, however both people gain new opportunities because they live in society.

Restricting the opportunity or possibility of oppressing is not restricting freedom in itself but restricting the use of power that would oppress one to generate an opportunity for another.

5. In a free society the people freely decide to carry out certain actions so that in collaboration with the other members of the society they can generate the society, circumstances, opportunities, and possibilities that they decided they wish to obtain through their social collaboration.

The formation of societies implies collaboration between human beings, the union of their effort, talent, intelligence, time, and capacities to achieve the desired objectives, to generate the circumstances sought by the members of society that will allow them to have the opportunities, possibilities, and freedoms that they decided to strive for when they developed their free society. Human beings freely decide what each of them or all of them are going to do together to achieve the objectives of the society, objectives which they themselves freely chose.

For example: the members of society can freely decide that to achieve the objective of having security, everyone will spend a certain amount of time out of their lives patrolling the streets of their city; or that in order to carry out certain projects together, everyone will give financial contribution or pay a tax to finance the project.

The development of a free society involves working together, not just sharing certain physical space. If the work that needs to be done to develop the society is freely decided on by all the members of a society, the society is free. If a powerful person or group determines that members of society have to carry out certain activities or work, then it is the use of power that determines what actions people have to take to belong to the society and not a free decision of all members of the society.

The difference between the development of free societies and the formation of oppressive societies is that in the free society people freely decide what they want to obtain from their society, what freedoms, opportunities, or powers they will limit or restrict, and what activities they will carry out to be able to belong and achieve the objectives of society. Whereas, in an oppressive society, a person or a group forces others to belong to the society and determines what other members of society can obtain by belonging to the society, what they have to do, and what they cannot do in order to belong to society.

An oppressive society occurs when a person or a group has the power to:

1. Coerce others to belong to the society.

2. Determine the circumstances that will be generated within the society.

3. Establish what each person obtains from the society.

4. Decide what each person has to do in order to belong to the society.

5. Determine what the people will not be able to do within society.

6. Exclude from society, take away freedom, exercise physical violence, and deprive members of the means of survival if they do not submit to the decisions of the powerful.

An oppressive society is developed when a person or a group of people control all or most of the economic resources, use of physical force and the political process, and therefore have the power to reduce the options of other people between starvation or depravation from the means of subsistence, being subjected to physical violence, being excluded from any type of society or submitting to the will of the powerful. In this case, submitting implies agreeing to act according to the wishes of the powerful and renouncing some of the freedoms and the possibilities generated by the formation of the society in order to stay alive with sustenance and to enjoy a minimum of the benefits that society generates.

An oppressive society is formed when some people use their power, be it political, physical, or of exclusive control of resources, to increase their own benefits, their own possibilities, opportunities, and freedoms, while reducing the benefits, opportunities, possibilities, and freedoms of the other members of the society.

A democratic society is one in which the members of a society do not use power to impose on others the rules of society, but one in which all members of society freely participate in the decision-making process that affect the members of the society.

CHAPTER 12

Private Decision vs Social Decision

A private decision is one that an individual person makes for his own life, and that affects him primarily, that does not require cooperation, consent, or agreement and that does not limit the freedoms and opportunities of other people.

The democratic social decision is a decision made by two or more people with the same power and value who are looking to cooperate, collaborate, or reach agreements to generate circumstances or to achieve a common objective, and to achieve it, they decide to do, or not to do some things in a voluntary way.

A social tyrannical decision is one which a person or a group make on their own accord and impose on others, without the consent of those affected; this decision will influence and affect the circumstances, freedoms, opportunities and lives of people who were not involved in the decision-making process, or who had less power to negotiate and leverage in the decision-making process.

In their private lives, each person decides, among the options, opportunities, and possibilities that their circumstances permit, what opportunities they are going to strive to generate for themselves, what actions they want to take to achieve the results and objectives they aspire to, in what areas of their lives they are going to restrict themselves or what desires and freedoms they are going to limit in order to be who they want to be and open the opportunities for which they are looking. In their private lives, each person decides, inside what their circumstances permit, what they strive for and what they will do and will not do to achieve it.

A free society is one in which all the members of the society have the same value and power to influence and determine the circumstances in which they live, the common objectives for their society, the social projects, the terms and conditions of the social contract, the freedoms, opportunities, possibilities, restrictions, limitations, and duties of all its members. A democratic society is one in which the individual decisions of all its members are equally taken into account to generate the social decisions that establish the reasons for which the society exists, the common objectives and projects every member of the society agrees on and for which they will collaborate and cooperate, what they have to do, or can't do, to generate the circumstances they aspire to have or to achieve their common objectives.

A tyrannical society is one in which a person or a group, through tyrannical social decisions decide the reason the society exists, the circumstances it will generate, the objectives of the society, the terms and conditions of the social contract, what they and every single person on the society will be allowed to do and not do.

A free society is not one in which every citizen can do absolutely whatever they desire to do when they have the power, the opportunity, and possibility to do it. Because in this case there is no society, there is only a common space where every person can make private decisions or tyrannical social decisions. In this case there will not be any mechanisms in place to limit the power of those who wish to oppress and there will not be any mechanisms in place through which agreements, cooperation, and collaboration can be achieved among the people who wish to generate a specific set of circumstances that will permit them to develop and generate opportunities, possibilities, and more freedoms for everyone involved. A space without democratic mechanisms and processes which is designed to reach agreements and to facilitate cooperation and collaboration is a space where the only societies that can develop will be based on power and all decisions will either be private or tyrannical social.

The diverse political and social systems are no more than different ways, processes, and institutions through which social decisions are made and executed. The democratic systems strive to empower every individual to make an individual decision, but at the same time they strive to give the same weight to every individual decision so that they cannot be imposed on the other members of the society. The democratic process is that which takes the individual decision of every citizen, gives them the same value and power, and turns them into a democratic social decision.

The search, our search, for the best democratic system, is the search for the most equitable, participatory, and efficient system to reach agreements, make decisions, and to generate and facilitate collaboration and cooperation. Such a system is a tool that can be used by the citizens to make any decision except that of oppressing the citizens. The system itself generates the circumstances in which the citizens live and develop because it limits oppression and empowers individuals to participate; and at the same time, it is the mechanism through which citizens make social decisions to determine their own circumstances.

CHAPTER 13

Freedom is the means and the end in itself

When human beings decide that the formation of a free society is one of their personal projects and they face other free human beings who have the same project; together they can develop a social system through which they will strive to establish a free society, and they decide the circumstances in which they wish to live and develop through this system, and the projects that they will undertake together, then the society, and everything that is done within it, is at the same time the means to achieve freedom and an achievement of freedom and an end in itself. For the free human being, the free society can be both the end in itself, that is, a shared life project, and the means by which he manages to generate the circumstances that allow him to have the possibilities and opportunities to develop his personal projects. The formation of a free society can be, in itself, a collaborative project that, in turn, manages to generate circumstances so that each member of the society can undertake individual projects thanks to these circumstances generated by the society.

The way in which a free society can be the final goal and the means in itself is similar to when a young person plans and has the life project of having and being part of a happy family. The ultimate end may be the happy family, but each step the young person takes and each action he takes to achieve this end is also the purpose and end for which he acts. Meeting potential partners, hanging out with one person or another, establishing a stable relationship, planning the future together, having children, etc., all these are actions to achieve the life project of belonging to a happy family, but every action can also be an achievement and a goal in itself, and every action is a part of life and of living. On the other hand, this project does not have an end and is not achieved at any time, but is lived in. The happy family project doesn't just involve having babies, being happy for a day, and dying. It involves a life plan, actions that are carried out day by day, satisfactions and dissatisfactions at all times, thousands of decisions, plans, and other projects within the main project. Therefore, the satisfaction of the life project is always in the present and in the future. The project can be satisfied at any time; and at the same time remain unsatisfied always, because as long as these human beings are alive they will have a future in which to aspire to be happy as a family, and being happy for a moment does not guarantee the happiness of future moments; each moment is living, it is the objective and it is a construction and a step to achieve the next objective and the next future.

Freely developing and building futures with other free human beings is one of the most rewarding activities that human beings can undertake. Because by doing so, he affirms his personal freedom, he is recognized and accepted by other free humans, he builds a project in common with them, and through the actions of his society, he influences his own circumstances; circumstances in which he will develop and which will expand his options, possibilities, and freedoms to develop and build his social and personal projects.

Do you want to live in a society that is not free, in which others determine all your circumstances, options, and possibilities without taking you into account? Do you want to live without forming societies with other human beings? Do you want to live in a society in which others have the opportunity to oppress you? Or do you want to live freely in a free society? What type of society would you like to build? What characteristics would you like your society to have? What would you ask members to refrain from doing in order to belong to your society? What would you like your society to be able to give to all of its members?

____

____

____

____

____

____

____

____

____

____

____

____

Do you think you can belong to or that you can develop, a free society that allows you and all other members of society to decide the reasons you have for being part of such society? How will all members of society collaborate? What does everyone have to do in order to achieve what you have all decided to strive for to generate the circumstances that will permit you to have and strive for your own personal life projects?

____

____

____

____

____

____

____

____

____

____

____

SECTION 3

Other Political Systems

In the last ten years I have come across many people who are angry or disappointed with the results that the system of electoral representative democracy has produced in their country; some of these people blame parties and politicians, others blame the system and call for a change in the system. Among those who blame the system, some propose other forms of democracy, systems that they consider to be truly democratic; others advocate for other systems in which few have all power and rule over many.

In this section of the book, we will analyze different forms of government, some democratic and others not so, to learn about the strengths and weaknesses of each system.

CHAPTER 1

Monarchy

The king rule over his subjects.

Monarchy is a system of government in which a person is the head of the state. Usually, this person came to his kingship position through violent conquest or he inherited the position from an ancestor who had obtained it through violent conquest.
Monarchs used to maintain their power and rule thanks to a combination of the following factors:

I.   Coercion through the threat and use of power.

The easiest and most primitive way used to incentivize and coerce people to comply with the laws of society is the threat and use of one or another type of power. When this happens, the society that is developed is not free.

Physical power is the capacity of a group to kill or inflict physical suffering over another person or group of people, the capacity to take away a person's possessions or means of subsistence, and to strip away a person or a group from their physical freedom of action and expression. This implies that anyone with power can reduce the options of persons with less power, so that they have to choose between obeying or losing their lives, suffering violence, losing their possessions or means of subsistence, or losing more freedoms and opportunities.

Since this authority is not based on the free acceptance of the law by the citizen, it is to be expected that, if the individuals have not been subjected by other means, they will look for ways to not comply with the law and avoid punishment. If coercion through power is the only motivation to follow a law, and the individual does not have enough fear, then he might decide not to follow the law. If the individual has a stronger emotion than fear, like hatred or greed, he will not follow the law. To maintain a society through coercion and power requires the expenditure of a lot of resources to maintain the population in a fearful state.

2.   The moral tradition and the indoctrination of subjects to obey authority.

This is possibly one of the greatest forces driving individuals to maintain the status quo of their society. The moral tradition can be passed from generation to generation, through specific and conscious codes or, more commonly, it can be passed down through experiences and examples, as a way of seeing the world and understanding the place of the individual within said world.

Much of the moral feeling that we humans have is conditioned in early childhood. What most people consider good or bad, their duties or their rights, their honor, their "value", is not usually the product of a conscious analysis but a conditioning generated in the subconscious of the human being who learns in childhood what the world is like and what is his place in it. Human beings are conditioned from early childhood to interpret themselves as someone who holds a place in society and who must act according to certain norms to maintain or better his social standing. Questioning social norms and one's own role in society can generate existential anguish, because questioning one's own social role means questioning one's own identity, and the meaning of one's life; and questioning social norms opens up boundless freedom, which is difficult to handle.

For example: while one person may consider it his evident and just duty and honor to dedicate his life to the unconditional service of a king, and even to lay down his life for the king, another person may feel that there is clearly no duty that compels another human being to unconditionally serve another human being, least of all a king.

The moral tradition comes from a predisposition of our organism to understand the world around us from an early age and to understand what is appropriate behavior for our survival and advancement. In a primitive society, ignoring instinct or community norms could put the individual and the entire community at risk of death. Our ability to think abstractly has reinforced the moral tradition by endowing it with arguments and justifications that go beyond practical, personal, or communal benefits, to the point where an instinctive mechanism that was developed to increase the survival of the individual and the community can now be used against that individual and the community to benefit a person or group.

Moral tradition can take the form of honor or duty, the desire to be a functional member within society, or the desire to climb the social hierarchy, or it can simply condition individuals in such a way that it would be very difficult for them to perceive themselves acting against the moral tradition.

Generation after generation, monarchs and ruling classes have preached and promoted submission and obedience as a virtue. The virtue of obedience and the virtue of submission have been so consistently preached over time that they have become a moral tradition. Respect and reverence for authority is a moral tradition presented as a virtue by authority itself. This virtue obviously benefits the person or people with power who are obeyed.

1. A religious character that was attributed to the king's reign.

People with power usually try to justify their power, and one of the ways they do that is through a religious character. The idea that God would decide who the monarch would be and that obeying the monarch was equivalent to obeying God gave strength to the moral argument to obey the king and justified the violence the king used to subject the people. This is extremely curious since most monarchs used to come to power through the use of violence or inheritance from an ancestor who became king thanks to the use of violence. If the above premise was true, God allows, encourages, and blesses the use of violence to achieve power.

Do you want a monarch who got his title thanks to the fact that he or his ancestors were the best killers, commanders of killers, and strategists of oppression, being the one who decides in what circumstances you live, what are your responsibilities, rights, and freedoms? Why?

____

____

____

____

____

____

____

____

____

____

Absolute Monarchy

In a society governed by an Absolute Monarch, the monarch has absolute power to decide and impose the objectives of the society, the projects, the goals, terms, and conditions of the social contract, everything allowed and prohibited, and all the circumstances of the society. In an absolute monarchy, there is no institution or group that can effectively curb the power of the monarch.

In simplified terms, the absolute monarch is the government of one who has the power to coerce others to belong to society, to decide what each one will get from the society, and what freedoms and rights they may and may not have. In an absolute monarchy, freedom is taken from all other human beings and they are oppressed, to give more power to the monarch.

In an absolute monarchy, the system and the decisions of the monarch determine absolutely all the circumstances in which the citizens will develop and face. Food security and the physical security of everyone in his kingdom depends on the monarch and the system. The monarch can be "good" and respect the lives of its citizens and have as its objective the generation of food and wealth for all. However; If the monarch is not "good" or "capable", there is no institution or power that can stop him and prevent him from abusing and oppressing all members of society.

The absolute monarch has the power to kill you, to steal from you, to demand taxes, to not give security or to control all aspects of your life.

In an absolute monarchy subjects are completely excluded from the decision-making process. This means that citizens have to live in the circumstances that are generated as a result of the monarch's decisions. That they cannot have an influence on the world in which their descendants will develop, face and live in. Must their circumstances depend on the monarch.

Some advocate absolute monarchy or something of the sort, arguing that it is a highly efficient system. What the monarch orders, is executed; therefore, it is effective in executing orders, since there is no considerable resistance to the king's commands, this could seem to make it a highly effective system. However, the inefficiency of the absolute monarchy system lies with the limitations of the monarch. If the monarch has a goal, but his knowledge and capabilities are limited (like that of all human beings), then he will develop plans and give orders to fulfill his objectives that are not really efficient or that have contrary consequences to his objectives. Granted there have been very gifted monarchs who manage to make the state apparatus work effectively to fulfill their objectives. This effectiveness can work both to fulfill an objective or project that the monarch considers "good" for the "people", or a project that the monarch considers "good" for him, even if it is "bad" for the "people". It should be emphasized that even when the monarch considers that an objective is "good for the people" the fact is he is not letting them participate in the political process, therefore he is oppressing them, controlling all their circumstances and forcing them to act and not to act in certain ways; No matter how much economic progress the monarch may give his subjects, by denying them their freedom he is treating them like a caged animal or an object, not like human beings with their own free will.

Furthermore, the monarch will most likely not be disinterested "saint" who establishes the objectives and laws of the State thinking about the well-being of his subjects, and without thinking about taking advantage of his position of absolute power to put his well-being, his interests and personal desires above those of his subjects. However, even if the absolute monarch is interested only in the fulfillment of what he considers his duty, and the duty he considers his own is the well-being of his subjects and of his nation, there is not and never has been an infallible human being. Even when the absolute monarch is trying to obtain something good for his people, since he is not infallible, his perception of the good of his people is probably wrong or at the very least limited. Because the monarch is not infallible and he has no one to stop him, his actions and legislation, even when they are the fruit of the best of intentions, may generate suffering for his subjects. With this system, the mistake of one person has devastating consequences for all.

An absolute monarch has absolute power over almost all the circumstances in which a human being develops, over politics, over the economy, over the law, over security, over infrastructure, etc.; in the circumstances created by this absolute monarch all his subjects are coerced to live.

Some claim to justify absolute monarchy with the romantic notion that the value of the monarch is such that it exceeds the value of all his subjects combined and therefore has the right to live fully himself, and to require his subjects to live in a limited way to benefit him. However, remember what gave the monarch absolute power and how he maintains it. The monarch obtains his power through oppression, conquest, the use of force or the position was inherited by him from those who used force to obtain and maintain it. Therefore if we accept the premise that the monarch is worth more than his subjects and he has the right to demand that they limit their intellectual capacities and freedoms to serve him, we are stating that the value of people and their right to be free humans is directly related to the amount of power they have and use to oppress others. If this is the case, we would consider that inventors, philosophers, writers, scientists, artists, and religious leaders and teachers are less valuable to humanity and should have fewer rights, opportunities, possibilities and freedoms than the human who has managed to amass large amounts of power over others and uses it to kill, limit and oppress others. If this were the case, we would have to consider Socrates, Christ and Buddha as inferior to Nero, Henry VIII and Hitler.

To be in favor of the absolute monarchy, or monarchy in general, is to be in favor of a society in which the freedom, development and capacities of all are limited and restricted to expand the freedom and power of the monarch; is to be in favor of the use of force to oppress and to value more the people who manage to oppress a large amount of humans. The more people they oppress the more valuable they are.

Do you want to live under an absolute monarchy?

____

____

____

____

____

____

Constitutional monarchy

Having recognized that the monarch is not infallible, that the moral or divine authority he has over his mandate are meaningless, that his interests may be contrary to those of the rest of society and that any action of his is oppressive to his subjects, in many countries, the union of nobles or commoners, whether through war, economic or other types of pressure, managed to impose limitations on the powers of the monarch and established a constitutional monarchy.

The constitutional monarchy is one in which the objectives of the society, the projects and terms and conditions of the social contract are established by negotiations between one monarch and another or other groups with power. The objective and the terms and conditions of the society are a balance between the interests of the monarch and the interests of the other group of people that unites to obtain a power comparable to that of the monarch. The power and functions of the monarch and the way of organizing the State are agreed between the monarch and other groups with power and placed on the constitution. In this type of social organization, the monarch is subject to the laws of the constitution, he usually has power over the citizens, but his power is limited by the laws.

Usually these groups are the nobles, the bourgeois, or the entire united population.

1.   Nobles:

When the nobles unite their military power to put legislative limits on the monarch.

This form of government recognizes that the monarch should not have absolute power over his subjects; but it does not do so out of consideration for all who are oppressed, but because a handful of subjects with large amounts of power, obtained through the use of force, violence and oppression, consider that the king has no absolute right over them; but that they and the king do have absolute power over all the other subjects therefore every criticism and argument against absolute monarchy applies to the constitutional monarchy when the constitution is agreed upon between the monarch's negotiations with groups of nobles.

2.   Bourgeois:

When the mercantile class manages to obtain enough economic power to face the power of the monarch, or of the monarch and the nobility, they can negotiate a constitution that protects their interests and gives them certain political powers.

This type of constitution is different from the previous one because in this case, those who negotiate did not necessarily gain power through the use of violence. However, it is a type of constitution that protects and gives power to a small percentage of the population and to a large extent maintains the power of the monarch. So, if not all, many of the arguments against absolute monarchy apply to the constitutional monarchy when the constitution is negotiated between the monarch and the bourgeois.

This continues to be a system that considers that whoever has more power has more value and more rights.

This is a system where those who are protected are the groups with power as long as they manage to maintain their power, but the interests, life, food, home, security of those who do not belong to the groups with power are not necessarily protected. Even if such a constitution might protect the lives of all citizens, it still considers some to be inferior to others and continues to limit their freedoms, opportunities and possibilities in favor of those of the monarch and the ruling classes.

This is a system in which a large part of the population is deprived of the opportunity to make decisions that alter their circumstances and their society; because that right is reserved for groups with power and they will surely put in the constitution their personal interests and not the interests of the population in general. Furthermore, even if they wanted to take into account the interests of the general population, they could hardly know them.

In this system, the majority of the population is being oppressed.

3.   The entire population:

Through the election of a parliament, citizens negotiate with the monarch and the nobles.

If in any way the members of a population vote for representatives who meet with the king and together develop a constitution, this constitution, at best, will be a balance between the interests of the monarch and the nobility and the interests of the population. By this point we would have already concluded that the monarch has no right to impose his will on all his subjects but he still holds power so considerable that his voice and vote equals that of all his subjects. This is a system in which one person has the same political weight as the rest of the population combined. The king has more value than every other citizen because his ancestors were better at killing, conquering and oppressing.

This is a type of government that basically says: Everyone is worth something, but one is worth more and must have greater power.

This is only an intermediate system between the idea that no one should have absolute power over others and the inability to completely remove people who obtained and maintained their power through violence and oppression.

Do you think that a single noble, monarch or bourgeois is worth the same as 100,000 or 1,000,000 citizens? Do you think the interests and criteria of one person should be more important than the interests of 100,000 or 1,000,000? Do you think that being a descendant of murderers, rapists, strategists of oppression, gives more value or wisdom to a person?

____

____

____

____

____

____

Parliamentary Monarchy

In theory, in a parliamentary monarchy, the only role of the monarch is ceremonial. However, the monarch and the nobles are allowed to keep their possessions, economic power and "honors" that their families managed to gather during the time they used violence to oppress their subjects. Not only is the monarch given a place of honor in society and is allowed to keep the wealth generated by oppression, but the citizens usually pay, through their taxes, to maintain the monarch and the nobles. Basically it is a system in which citizens are told that they may have control of the state but that they have to revere and pay money to maintain the luxurious lives of the descendants of those who oppressed their ancestors. Not only is this the case, but the vast majority of the time, the idea that the king is just a ceremonial figure ends up being a lie, he retains at least some political and economic power.

For example in England the legislative power is divided into two. The House of Lords and the House of Commons. Members of the House of Commons are voted for by citizens and members of the House of Lords are the descendants of nobles who wish to participate. This means that the descendants of the oppressors of society have the power to create or stop laws that will affect the lives of all individuals in the country.

Furthermore, even if in reality the figure of the monarch is merely a symbolic one, the symbol of the monarch is a harmful one for the members of a society who wish to live freely. Because it is the symbol that some are considered more valuable because their ancestors were better at killing and oppressing.

Do you think it's fair that part of your taxes go to maintain the luxurious lifestyle of the descendants of the murderers and oppressors of your ancestors? Do you think it is fair to honor these people?

____

____

____

____

____

____

____

____

Electoral Monarchy

Electoral Monarchy is the rule of the elected monarch. Some ancient kingdoms elected their kings. The citizens or the aristocracy got together to vote for a king. There were many different types of elected monarchies. On some of them, the power of the monarch was limited by a constitution, or by the power of the aristocrats themselves. Other elective monarchies gave almost unlimited power to the king. This form of government, granted power to one person to rule over everyone. It is an intermediary system developed to hold two opposing ideas in one system: The idea that some deserve to have all the power and rule over everyone, and the idea that everyone should be able to participate in the decisions that affect their lives. Electoral monarchies are born from the tension between the idea that everyone should have the right to decide and participate in the decisions that affect their lives, and the idea that some people have inherent qualities that make them superior to all others, that some people deserve more freedom and power than others, and that the "masses" should be controlled. This tension is still present and is institutionalized in the Roman Republic, and now in all modern republics.

Electoral monarchy is a system of government that organizes society so that the citizens can choose who will have all the power and govern them.

Do you want to vote to give power to a king? Do you want to vote to give power to someone to rule over you? Do you want to vote to give power to someone to decide how your society will be? Do you want to vote to give power to someone to decide what options will be available to you, the circumstances in which you will live, the benefits, freedoms, restrictions, and responsibilities you will have?

____

____

____

____

____

____

____

____

____

CHAPTER 2

Aristocracy

The rule of the nobility over the subjects.

Talking about monarchies automatically leads us to talk about the aristocracy. The aristocracy is a social class that is above the other social classes, has more political power, and usually has economic and military power as well. A person does not become part of the aristocratic class simply by amassing economic, political, or military power, usually a series of rituals and requisites are needed to elevate the simple warlord, the wealthy merchant, or whoever has political talent to be part of the aristocracy. These requisites were decided by those who were already part of the aristocratic class, who inherited their status in this class. These requirements are completely arbitrary and designed to elevate aristocrats to a "more than human" status. However, almost all aristocrats became so simply because their ancestors were effective in organizing killers and oppressors, but not so effective that they became kings. Their power enabled them to rule and oppress many, but not all. Their power gave them a noble title that they then passed down from generation to generation. To justify their inherited power and position, subsequent generations of aristocrats invented a mythology that gave greater "ontological", "natural", "by birth" value to their descendants rather than to non-descendants of aristocrats.

There are those who are in favor of the aristocracy, arguing that society should be governed by the most capable people with the best qualities, and that aristocrats are the people with the best qualities.

However, a minimal amount of analysis leads to the conclusion that the inheritors of the aristocracy are not possessors of any better qualities. The only qualification necessary to become a noble in the early Middle Ages was to be the best at killing, or organizing killers to conquer and oppress. When the nobles of European countries could no longer use their countrymen to brutally oppress one another, they used them to conquer colonies in which they exploited or killed local populations.

When the aristocracy has had power, they have murdered, conquered, exploited, and oppressed its own population and/or the population of other countries. If the remaining descendants from nobles and aristocrats really were people of extraordinary qualities who were guided not by self-interest, but by the common good of society, then they would apologize on behalf of the atrocities their ancestors committed, resign, and return their fortune to the citizens from their own countries and from the countries colonized by them; otherwise, they will not have demonstrated that their interests are "the good of all" and not just their personal good, and they would not have demonstrated that they have superior capacities over those of the rest of the population, except for the ability to take advantage of circumstances, the system, power, and of their subjects to achieve personal gain.

As in a monarchy, in an aristocracy the circumstances of the subjects are decided or influenced by aristocrats. The economy, violence, peace, war, crime, the amount of wealth, the food available, the taxes, all are determined or influenced by the aristocrats, usually to favor themselves. As in a monarchy, ordinary human beings, their time, their work, their effort, serve only to empower the nobles. Ordinary human beings can only do what the nobles allow. Their lives are directly dependent on the nobles. Aristocrats oppress other human beings and they limit the freedoms and opportunities of other humans to gain power and opportunities for themselves. The same arguments that we used against the monarchy, we can use against the aristocracy.

The aristocracy of people with the best qualities

If one wanted to argue, as many do, that the people with the best qualifications should be in power, the first thing that would need to be done would be to define these qualities, and there would be as many definitions of "good qualities" as there are free-thinking human beings. However, the first thing most of us will agree on is that being a descendant of noble murderers and oppressors does not give a person higher qualities. If anything, the opposite would be true.

If we wanted to explore new ways to decide who the people with the best qualities are, the question would have to be asked: Who are the people with the best qualities? The businessmen? All of them? Does that include Nazi businessmen, weapons and armament business owners, Chinese businessmen, Americans, Trump, Bill Gates, or who among the businessmen has this higher qualities? Are the people with the best qualities the people with the most money? Those who own land or pay a certain amount of taxes? Maybe the philosophers are the people with the greatest qualities? But all of them? Including Epicurus, Marco Aurelio, Nietzsche, Sartre, and Derrida, or which ones? Are the people with the higher qualities the peasants and the workers? Who among them? Are the people with the higher qualities the ones that studied the most in society? Are they those who studied a specific career and got the best grades? But what career and in which school and who has access to this school? Are they the most empathetic? But according to what criteria? And is that the only quality? Can the highest qualities be measured alongside a person's IQ? But IQ does not determine the degree of empathy or values or ethics, worldview, or moral character of a person. Who determines what qualities people have to possess to be considered "of high qualities", and therefore should rule over all of us?

The question in this case is not only about the monarchy or aristocracy, but in general. Why does a human being have rights over other human beings? Why are one or a handful of human beings the only ones with the right to expand their freedom, opportunities, and power while reducing the freedoms, opportunities, and power of everyone else? Why do a few have the right to decide what the world will be, and the circumstances in which all will develop and live? Why is one human being more valuable than another or many other human beings? Why does a human being have the right to decide under what circumstances all other human beings will live? Why can one human being compel another human being to obey him? Why can a human being, or a group, limit and oppress the freedoms of other human beings?

What "high qualities" would justify elevating one human so much above all other humans? Who decides which men have the highest qualities? Who empowers these "higher qualities" humans? Why does the possession of these high qualities give a group of human beings the right to limit the freedom and determine the circumstances in which all other human beings will live?

The objection in this case is not that all human beings have the same qualities, but that all human beings have the same right to be complete human beings; to develop their inner world freely and without restrictions, to establish their own life goals, to establish their own personal and social projects, to strive in the world to carry out their personal and social projects; to be part of the decisions that affect their life. If a human being is oppressed, his or her humanity is being taken away, he is being reduced to being a slave, a tool, a pack animal, a caged animal, or an object.

Furthermore, in all types of aristocracy, a select group of people are empowered to control the lives of the rest of the population and by doing so they are empowered to work for their personal interests, one of which would be the consolidation of the social structure that allows them to have power over others and that allows them to fully develop as humans while oppressing the rest of the population. Even if all aristocrats were selfless saints, they would still be oppressors.

Now decide: Do you think that because Aristocrats are descendants of murderers and oppressors they are worth more or have better qualities than you? Do you think that by having some specific qualities, others have the right to take away your freedoms? Do they have the right to prohibit you from influencing the world around you? Do you think that they have the right to determine all the circumstances in which you will develop? Do you think others should make all, or some of the decisions that affect your circumstances, and your life? Do you want to live ruled by the descendants of murderers and oppressors? Do you want to live ruled by a handful of people who consider themselves to have "better qualities" than you?

CHAPTER 3

Dictatorship

The government of one or some with most of the power in society over others who have little or no power.

A dictatorship consists of a unified government under the command of a person or a powerful group which does not allow and punishes opposition and dissent.

A dictatorship can be achieved through the use of military or economic power or through popular election in an electoral representative democracy.

1.   Through military power:

A person or group uses its military power to remove the government and establish itself as the head of the State. Dictators usually remove all opposition through the use of force. The elimination of the opposition, in these cases, is almost entirely done by the use of military and police force, assassination and imprisonment of those who supported the previous government, of the dissidents, and of any group of people who do not submit.

2.   Through elections:

In an electoral representative democracy, instances will inevitably develop in which an individual or a group obtains power through elections, and that once in power, they modify the constitution to expand their power and make use of their power to obtain more power, to eliminate dissent, and to make it impossible for the opposition to win elections, becoming dictators. In these cases, dictators often work for the interests or ideas of one part of the population, while subduing and eliminating dissent, the opposition, and other parts of the population.

The problems of electoral representative democracy such as polarization can lead to the radicalization of certain groups in society, and this can incentivize them to justify the oppression of the sector of the population that they consider to be enemies. It is natural, but not inevitable, for electoral representative democracies to breed dictators.

Even when the dictator comes to power through a popular election, and even if the majority of the population continues to support him throughout his dictatorship, the fact that he uses his power to expand his powers beyond what was initially permitted, and to oppress and eliminate dissent, opposition, and minorities makes him a dictator.

Dictators usually come to govern or retain government through the use of power. Their power is so superior to that of all other members of society that the dictator can make all the decisions that affect all members of society, establishing the objectives of society and how they will be achieved and, in doing so, they is responsible for all circumstances within society.

Usually in a dictatorship the life, freedom, economic and social standing of citizens depend 100% on their adherence to the regime, and even in these cases, their lives may not be assured. Dictators tend to justify their oppressive actions saying they are necessary sacrifices for the good of the State or the people who constitute the majorities. However, regardless of how small a minority is, it is still a group of human beings. Oppression, murder, or "sacrifice" of human beings for the particular idea that the dictator holds of what is "good for the state" does not justify the suffering, oppression, or murder of human beings. Oppression from the majorities to the minorities continues to be oppression.

Even if the dictator has the "common good" as an objective, his definition of the common good may be contrary to that of other people, and so he might end up working for an ideal of the common good that is oppressive for some citizens. But even when the majority of citizens, or the groups with power and the dictator have the same ideal of what the common good is, due to the fact that it is a dictatorship, the decision-making process excludes most citizens, and the execution of decisions oppresses most citizens; Regardless of any ideal or action taken by the dictator, the system itself is oppressive because it submits humans to authority. Even if the goal is the common good, the means or methods by which the dictator achieves this supposed common good are oppressive and dehumanizing.

There are those who argue that human beings must have their freedom taken away for their "own good". However, this argument removes freedom from the equation of what is "good" for the human being, and it takes away the possibility that freedom itself is not only something that is "good for the human" but that freedom is a characteristic of the human. If what is good for humans is opposed to their freedom, perhaps the best society would be one in which each human being lived in a cage and machines gave them everything they needed to eat. In this way, each human being would have what it takes to survive and would live "safely". However, a human being is not a computer that only requires energy. A human being is not an animal that will be "better" if he is caged and suffers neither physical violence nor hunger. This book will not go into details about what makes human beings human, nor on the moral, ethical, and philosophical character of freedom, but we can easily arrive at the simple conclusion that without freedom, economic prosperity, physical security and nutrition are not a "good" for the human being. Physical security and food are only needs that, if covered, allow us to live life for the purpose or the reason we freely decide. But physical security, safety, and food are not, in themselves, what gives meaning to human life. We require food to stay alive, but food in itself is not the purpose for which humans live, just as we require air to stay alive, but air in itself is not the purpose of a life. We have to be careful not to mistake what is needed to stay alive with what a human's life and life's purpose is about.

In a dictatorship, citizens have to live in the circumstances that the decisions and actions of dictators generate; they cannot have an influence on the world in which they live and must face each day and the circumstances in which their children will be born, develop, live in. All their circumstances depend on the dictators, any attempt to go against the dictators usually has serious consequences such as the loss of physical, economic, or food security, or the restrictions of more freedoms. Human beings in a dictatorship only have the freedoms that the dictators let them have, they reduce their agency to obey or be punished.

Some argue that a dictatorship is a more efficient system than democracy, yet dictators often fill positions of power with friends and family they consider loyal, not the most capable or fit because in a dictatorship, the loyalty to people with power is the most necessary requirement to maintain the social hierarchy's power. This simple fact makes dictatorships the perfect systems to oppress, but not necessarily the best to execute and achieve the objectives of dictators, because the most important requirement to move up in a dictatorship's hierarchy is loyalty and not competence. This is a system that could be efficient if the members of the dictatorial organization are intelligent and capable and they all have a single objective. Usually, the common goal they have is to establish a strict and fixed social order in which some are oppressed and others are uplifted or the idea of the State is exalted. This means that even if the dictatorial system is effective, the first thing it will be effective in is in eliminating the freedom of its citizens.

In a dictatorship, the social structure sacrifices the freedoms and opportunities of the individuals and potentiates and expands the freedom and power of the dictators. For an idea of the "common good" or "good of the State", dictators often sacrifice not only freedom but welfare and even the lives of the population. In a dictatorship, the time, life, talent, and effort of every citizen is at the service of the State and/or the dictator. In this social organization, it is not the state that is at the service of the individuals, but the individuals that are at the service of the state.

Perhaps through the government of a dictator, the economy can be controlled and expanded to generate a certain prosperity, at least for certain social classes, but economic growth is not the purpose of a human society. If anything, economic growth is the means to obtain more human freedoms, opportunities, and possibilities. If repression, violence, and oppression are used to achieve economic growth, economic growth is considered more valuable than the human being, his freedom, and his humanity. Through economic growth, a human can get better food to sustain himself, but if he has no freedom to decide what he wants to do with the life he sustains, then that life becomes meaningless.

Some people consider that a dictator is necessary to solve the problems of electoral representative democracy. But the dictatorship can only increase these problems, not reduce them. If, in an electoral representative democracy, the people compete in order to be represented, and therefore the oppressors of those who are not going to be represented and are going to be oppressed. In a dictatorship, everyone is always oppressed. Some might think that a dictator who thinks like they do would be the solution to a nation's problems, but even these people may recognize that it is impossible for a dictator to think as they do in every respect; therefore the dictator will end up imposing laws or carrying out actions that the person who supported him considers unjust or bad.

The dictator cannot think 100% the same as you do, so he will make decisions that are contrary to what you think or believe in and will eventually end up oppressing you.

Do you think you and the dictator will have the same opinions in everything? Do you think that your ideas and opinions should be imposed on thousands and millions of people? That your idea of fairness, justice, or the economy are worth more than the freedom of all other human beings? Do you think that the idea a person has on what is the best way to run or rule society should be imposed on every single person?

CHAPTER 4

Epistocracy

The government of the knowledgeable.

Epistocracy is the idea that knowledgeable people are the ones who should rule. There are different ways of applying an epistocracy, but the basic principle is that whoever has the knowledge should have the control or power.

When facing this form of social organization, the first thing we must ask ourselves is: Knowledge of what and according to whom? There is a great deal of knowledge in the world; some have knowledge about psychology, others about economics, others about agriculture, others about ancient cultures, others about the sufferings that the lower classes face. Others have a degree that ensures that they have specific knowledge, others study on their own and others learn empirically. What kind of knowledge is valid? The person or groups that determine what is the "valid and useful knowledge" determine the objectives of the entire society because by determining that a specific knowledge is more valuable than other types of knowledge they are determining that what could be achieved through that knowledge or the point of view held by the people with that knowledge is the objective society should strive for. If someone determines that the knowledge required to make decisions that will affect all members of society is economic knowledge, then the implicit goal of society will be economic growth. The person or group that determines the type of knowledge necessary to govern is determining the objectives and, to a certain extent, the direction of their society.

Another question that has to be asked when facing an epistocracy is: In addition to knowledge, is it necessary for a person to have a specific point of view and stand regarding that knowledge? For example, a person may know the basics of the different philosophical schools but consider only one of them to be the correct one. Those who consider Stoicism to be the best philosophy will make very different decisions than those who believe that the Epicureans had the answer, or those who ascribe to Nietzsche's philosophy of power. Those who adopt Camus' existentialism of the absurd will make very different decisions than those who ascribe to De Beauvoir's existentialist philosophy of freedom. Knowing about philosophy, having a degree in philosophy, tells us nothing about the philosophical positions of a person.

The socialist, liberal, neoliberal, capitalist, and communist economists all may have certain knowledge in common but some will lean towards one or the other political and economic philosophy. In an epistocracy, is it knowledge or posture according to knowledge that determines whether or not a person has power? If it is decided that economists should make a country's decisions, will it be Marxist economists, capitalists, socialists, or which of all the other options? Even if it is decided that they are capitalist economists, then one has to inquire if they are from Friedrich Hayek's school, John Maynard Keynes' school. Or are they Neo-Liberals or do they follow the recommendations of Modern Monetary Theory.

Usually it is not only the lack of information that leads some to call others ignorant, but the fact that they have opposite positions. For example, many who watch right-wing news channels often regard those who watch left-wing news channels as ignorant, and the reverse is also true. They might all share information but not a point of view or a common interpretation of such a point of view.

Another question that we have to ask ourselves when facing the epistocracy is: Does having knowledge make a person have more capacity to distinguish good and evil or to always decide according to the common good? Having knowledge has no moral implication.

That is, knowledge is information and in the case of the epistocracy, literally power, what is done with this information and with this power, does not depend on the power itself, but on what the person considers just, good or bad, their objectives and the moral character of the person.

It is enough to study a little bit of history to know that the people or social classes with knowledge are not necessarily the most humanitarian. The nobility of all kingdoms used to have a better understanding of philosophy, language, politics, art, and literature than their subjects, and indeed this difference usually justified the constant oppression of "the ignorant". The colonizing countries usually called themselves "civilized" and their "knowledge and education" justified oppression and killings.

For example: the top Nazi and fascist officers under Mussolini and Franco were "educated" and highly "knowledgeable" people, and they were also the most famous mass murderers and oppressors of the 20th century.

The fact that a person has knowledge of economics does not mean that his objective will be economic prosperity for every member of the society, or that part of his goal will be to reduce the economic inequality of members of society. Furthermore, knowledge of one subject does not make someone familiar with all subjects, with the lives and interests of all persons. On the other hand, the knowledge that a person possesses has nothing to do with his empathy or compassion. The fact that a person has certain knowledge and power does not ensure that he understands the common good or that he acts seeking the good of other members of society.

Another question essential to face the epistocracia is: who has more knowledge than myself about my circumstances, my desires, and my life projects? With this, what I mean is that although a person has academic knowledge on one or another subject, he does not have practical knowledge about the life, the circumstances, the desires, and the projects of all other individuals in the society. An economist can make decisions that will increase a country's GDP, but his method could destroy the way of life of farmers, workers, and craftspeople or have devastating ecological consequences.

A person or group of people may think that having time to be with their friends and family, or time for art and creativity or in nature, is more important for them than working to generate more money; but if the objective of the rulers is to raise the GDP, then they will surely generate circumstances in which people have to work more and spend less time with nature, friends, culture, family, art, etc. Your own goals and desires are not the goals and desires of all other humans.

Another question to ask when confronting the idea of epistocracy is: Why do some people have knowledge and others do not? This question is very important since it determines who has the power and the right to be free in a society.

Generally, most of the people who achieve academic degrees are members of the middle, upper middle, and upper class, as they usually have the resources to pay for education and/or to not have to work to support themselves and their families during the period when they are dedicated to study. In the current circumstances, in which only members of the middle and upper social classes have access to a certain type of education, if an epistocracy were instituted, an aristocracy would automatically be generated, increasing inequality of power and freedom and justifying it through the ideas of knowledge and ignorance.

The epistocracy reduces the possibilities for those who do not have the specific knowledge deemed to be useful, to that previously held by the subjects of a monarchy, or by the women before they could vote and run for office. Because they lack a specific knowledge, they are not allowed to partake in the decision-making process that determines the circumstances in which they live.

To criticize the epistocracia is not to criticize the idea that certain people are better able to perform certain jobs or to achieve certain objectives. To criticize the epistocracy is to criticize the idea that knowledge automatically turns a person into a being who will strive for the common good and not for personal benefit. To criticize the epistocracy is to criticize the idea that only a sector of the population has the capacity to establish the objectives, projects, and circumstances of the entire society. To criticize epistocracy is to criticize the idea that one type of knowledge is more valuable than another when determining the objectives of society when generating the circumstances in which all members of society will live and develop.

Do you think that the knowledge, objectives, and projects of an indigenous person have less value than the knowledge, objectives, and projects of an engineer who works for an international car manufacturer or that of the son of a millionaire? Do you think that by having certain knowledge and titles, the son of a rich person will know what is "best" for the indigenous person in the mountains, what he wants to do with his life, etc.? Do you think that because someone has a degree or more knowledge in a specific area, they should have the right to decide the circumstances that you are going to face?

____
____
____
____
____
____
____
____
____
____
____
____
____
____
____
____
____
____

CHAPTER 5

Technocracy

The government of technicians.

Technocracy is the government of technicians, but more widely interpreted, the government of specialists. Under this system, specialists in each sector of government and public life hold the power.

With this social organization system, a health specialist would be in charge of the healthcare system, a technology specialist in telecommunications, an economy specialist would be in charge of the country's economy, etc. This type of social structure, like many others, skips the process of determining the goals of society and proposes a system in which the goals of society appear to have been accepted in advance. However, to be able to choose which specialists are needed and the amount of power and preference they will have, it is necessary to decide the objectives of the society first. Because to organize a technocracy, a value system with an objective or goal hierarchy is necessary. A person specialized in a specific area is hired to head such an area because such an area is deemed important for the advancement of society. The technocracy, in itself, is just a way in which society can strive to achieve specific goals. It is not a system through which society can determine its goals and objectives. On the other hand, having technical knowledge about a subject does not determine the moral character of the technician, or that he has the capacity to determine what is just, or the right to decide the circumstances in which all human beings in his society will develop. Against the idea of technocracy, in general, we can apply the criticisms we made against epistocracy.

Technocracy of businessmen

Some claim that the people best capable of governing a society are the businessmen who have managed their companies in such a way that they have maximized profits and achieved great company growth. The argument is that if these corporate managers have been successful in corporate governance, they will be successful in social governance. This means that businessmen are the ones who establish the objectives of society and the projects and action plans to achieve these objectives that will generate the circumstances in which citizens live and develop.

Businessmen have been successful in governing their companies with very specific objectives, terms, and conditions; therefore, if the objectives, terms, and conditions of society are the same as those of companies, then it is reasonable to think that businessmen could succeed in governing society. However, let us reflect on what the objectives, terms, and conditions of a company are.

Objectives: The objectives of a company are measured primarily in economic terms, usually without taking cultural, social, ecological, or human factors into consideration. The main objective of a company is to maximize profits for the owners of the company. This means that business managers would only have more experience and training than other people in achieving the economic objectives of a society; furthermore, they only have experience in generating wealth for the owners, for a few people, not everyone in their companies. If the goal of society is the equitable economic benefit and success of all its citizens, a business manager no longer has the training or proper experience to accomplish this goal. If the objectives of the society are to foment the intellectual, social, cultural, and personal development of its citizens, then the director of a company is no longer the person best equipped to guide that society. Furthermore, a businessman works in a company that has its primary objectives set beforehand and is not prepared to decide the objectives of the whole of society. In a business, the objectives are usually very clear cut: to generate wealth for the owners. In a society, choosing the society's objectives is one of the main purposes of the political process.

Terms and conditions: The terms and conditions for a company are very specific and totalitarian: Those from above decide, those from below execute, and dissent is punished with dismissal. In a company and in a corporation, authority is completely vertical and descends from owners to directors, from directors to managers, to supervisors, to workers, and criticism of authority is punished. This means that a company director is only qualified to govern a totalitarian state where his authority is not questioned, where everyone executes his mandates, and where dissent can be punished. Otherwise, he is not the person best qualified to govern. A business director is only qualified to govern under a totalitarian system and, therefore, we can criticize this type of government with the same criticism we used against other forms of totalitarian governments such as dictatorships.

Do you think you should be governed by businessmen? Do you think that the sole objective of society should be to generate wealth for a small group of people? Do you think that everyone in the society should obey businessmen? Do you want your governor to behave like your boss?

____

____

____

____

____

____

____

____

____

____

____

____

____

Technocratic scientists

Some people also hold the idea that those who are better able to guide a society are scientists. When faced with this proposal, we have to be very careful not to mistake every engineer, chemist, and medic for a scientist, since many of them are merely technicians in their disciplines and not scientists. That is, they do not follow the scientific method to investigate and discover information from the physical world. Most medics, engineers, chemists, etc., have learned certain principles and apply them without making extensive use of the scientific method. Using the tools or knowledge developed by science does not make you a scientist; the scientist is only the one who uses the scientific method, and he is only a scientist when he is using such method.

On the other hand, it should also be noted that the objective of the scientific method is to understand the natural world and, in itself, has no other value or objective than the obtainment of information from the natural world. The application of the information obtained using the scientific method depends on the objectives of those who hold the power and knowledge.

For example: Scientific information can be used to develop nuclear bombs, nuclear power, radiation therapy, or radiographs. The scientific information is similar, but the application that is given to scientific information depends on the objectives of the scientists or engineers or of those who hired them.

The information that leads to the development of a medicine to cure a disease can be used to eradicate the disease and to reduce human suffering, or to generate economic profits for a company that sells the medicine at very high prices. The application that is given to information and discovery depends on the objectives of those who have the knowledge and the power to apply the knowledge.

Scientists and those who have the technical knowledge to apply the knowledge and tools developed by the scientific method, have knowledge and tools that could be very useful in achieving some of the objectives of some societies. Information about the natural world is a tool that can be used in many ways and for many purposes. The use of the scientific method is a tool, not an end in itself. Scientists can help achieve the objectives of a society and can provide information that helps a society determine its goals, projects and how to execute them, but they have no greater capacity than other individuals to develop value judgments that determine the objectives or the moral character of a society.

Do you think that scientists should decide the reasons why you belong to a society, what society will give you, what society will forbid you, the freedoms you will and will not have, etc.? Or do you think that science should be a tool to achieve the objectives of the society?

____
____
____
____
____
____
____
____

Technocracy of Lawyers

Another form of technocracy that is usually proposed is the government by lawyers. The argument put forward is that they are the ones who know the law best and have dedicated their lives to the study of justice. This could work if the concept of justice was a static one and if the laws did not require updates, modifications, changes, or to be eliminated entirely. Lawyers are only trained to deal with the established law and to interpret the law under their moral perception, their personal interests, and those of their clients. But as justice, morality, and the objectives of human beings are concepts that evolve over time, lawyers are not more capable than any other citizen to understand their evolution. The qualifications of lawyers might make them experts in present and past laws, however, that does not mean that they are the best persons to determine new laws or that they have the right to choose the objectives of society, the laws, freedoms, responsibilities, and obligations of citizens and the circumstances in which they will develop and in which all individuals will live.

Do you think lawyers are the people who should decide what is just, fair, and moral? Should they decide what freedoms and obligations you will have? To determine the circumstances in which you are going to live? Or the benefits your society will give you?

____
____
____
____
____
____
____
____

Technocracy in general

The argument against technocracy is not that there are no people more capable than others to perform certain actions or to make certain decisions. Rather, it is that these people do not have the right to decide and determine the objectives of a society, what is permitted and prohibited, the opportunities, possibilities and freedoms of all members of society and the circumstances under which all human beings will develop and live. In this case, the criticism is not to determine who is more or less capable of achieving an objective, but who has the right to determine the society's objective. Because if the members of a society cannot determine the objectives of their society, they are not free.

Do you think that someone else should decide what society is going to give you, the circumstances that society is going to generate, the benefits it is going to give you, what it is going to demand of you, and what freedoms society will restrict?

____

____

CHAPTER 6

Meritocracy

The government of those with merits.

There are many types of meritocracies in the world, but the basic idea is the same for all. A meritocracy is a system in which an individual can move up the social or political hierarchy when he achieves a certain merit. The justification is that if a person has achieved certain merits that others have not achieved, then this person has more abilities or is more dedicated and therefore he must be rewarded because he has the abilities to hold one or another type of power over those who did not achieve the merits.

If you achieve something, you have a reward. If you achieve something, it is because you have more qualities than others and therefore you should have power over them.

Initially, meritocracy was an idea that went against the aristocracy and was presented as a fairly progressive idea. Because instead of establishing that power, money and government would be inherited and transferred from father to son, it established that a person should be rewarded on his own merits.

In a meritocracy, the objective of the members of the society is usually to move up in the hierarchy by means of their merits; and thanks to their merits they justify the power they have over other members of society because they believe that they deserve it.

In a meritocracy, those with power justify themselves and the system with the following argument:
"I have my position thanks to my accomplishments. You have not gained my level in the social hierarchy because you have not tried hard enough or because you are not a capable person, therefore I am better than you and I deserve your obedience."

When confronted with the idea of meritocracy, we have to ask ourselves a couple of questions: Who determines what merits are necessary to move up in the hierarchy and obtain the rewards? Who determines the objectives towards which these merits are directed?

In a corporation, the merits necessary to move up the hierarchy are established by the director of the company and are focused on achieving a single objective: generating economic profit for the company. However, in a society, who defines the objectives of the society and the merits necessary to move up in the social hierarchy? What are these objectives and these merits?

Another very important question to ask is: Do all human beings in a meritocracy start with equal circumstances and opportunities, or do some have a competitive advantage? In the world in which we human beings currently live, we do not start with equal opportunities and circumstances. Some people come from privileged circumstances that permit them to obtain better education than others, and to dedicate more time, effort, and energy to studying and training to achieve the merits of the meritocracy. This gives them an advantage to climb the social hierarchy. The reality is that in the vast majority of cases, those who manage to climb up the social hierarchy usually start with a competitive advantage that gives them the possibility to dedicate themselves 100% to the objective of climbing the social hierarchy; and they usually have more opportunities due to their privileged education and their social capital. Due to the circumstances of birth, some people will have more obstacles and others more opportunities, therefore this remains a system that gives an advantage to the most powerful social classes because the "merits" a person of high class need to achieve to "deserve" a high social position or to "merit" power, are much less than the "merits" that a lower class person has to achieve. A real meritocracy is only possible when every person starts in the same circumstances and has the same opportunities.

In a meritocracy people can usually move up the social hierarchy through outstanding effort. Usually this involves spending more time and effort than the other members of society to achieve the "merits" to climb the social hierarchy. This turns the meritocracy into a race to dedicate more and more time in the life of each human being to achieving the merits of the meritocracy, otherwise they will remain in the lower hierarchies and will be ruled by others. This makes a meritocracy a system that encourages human beings to abandon their personal goals and projects in favor of the system's goals. The human being who does not wish to be subdued and governed by others, who wishes to have "value" within his society, must abandon all personal objectives and dedicate himself to obtaining the merits necessary to rise in the social hierarchy.

If, in a meritocracy, all members of society are asked to work eight hours a day, it is likely that whoever wants to gain the "merits" will work eight and a half hours, if the others do not want to lag behind they will have to voluntarily work eight and a half hours, then whoever wants to excel will have to work nine hours, then nine and a half hours, then ten, twelve or more hours a day, then work on weekends and so on. This will turn work and the effort to rise in the social hierarchy into the only socially acceptable and laudable objective for people in the meritocracy.

The meritocratic system rewards people whose sole objective is to move up the social hierarchy. Personal relationships, enjoying life, having personal projects different from those requested by the meritocracy, having objectives other than those of the meritocracy, go against dedicating more and more time, effort, and talent to the objectives and merits of the meritocracy.

Meritocracy rewards those who start with a competitive advantage and those who make climbing the hierarchy their only goal or the biggest objective of their lives. People who do not dedicate their entire lives to obtaining the necessary merits to obtain power, are ruled over, and the goals of their society, the laws, the circumstances, and everything in society will be decided by the people who reject everything in life except climbing the social hierarchy.

In a meritocracy, empathy and solidarity are often rejected in favor of self-interest and using people as a means of achieving the necessary merit to level up.

In the world we live in today, there is a meritocracy of which the goal is economic gain. Whoever has more economic power can influence or determine the circumstances of all the members of society. Those with the greatest economic power are those who have inherited it, those who had the opportunity to study and prepare in better universities, those who have contacts that give them opportunities, those who are better at exploiting the work of others and the natural resources, and those who dedicate every effort in their lives to the generation of wealth. These people reject everything, or almost everything, in their personal lives to obtain economic wealth or to obtain power. In the meritocracy, the person who rejects everything but the goals of the meritocracy is valued and given more power in order to generate more money and power. The person who does not pay attention to his family, friends, and personal life because he is dedicating himself to generating money is considered smarter, wiser, and worthy of power.

On the other hand, a meritocracy does not necessarily have as an objective the preservation and flourishing of human life or the freedom of humans. The objectives and the established merits determine whether or not the meritocracy will be one that protects the life of human beings and their freedoms. The meritocratic system tends to justify the inequality and the shortcomings of the lower classes by asserting that it is their own fault because they have not worked hard enough to earn the merits to climb the hierarchy or that they are inferior. This idea justifies perpetuating and enlarging social inequality from generation to generation, since those who are not at the top of the hierarchy are blamed for being inferior and not trying hard enough, and therefore for having less power and opportunities for themselves and their children. Everything, from the type of food to the opportunities available to each sector and social class is usually defined by its position within the meritocracy. Whoever has a good position within the meritocracy has access to good food, whoever does not have a good position may suffer deficiencies or only have access to food lacking in nutrients. The only way for a meritocracy to ensure nutritious food for all members of society is if food is one of the express objectives of society. But in the meritocracy of capitalism, the objective of society is to generate wealth for the people in the upper echelons of the social hierarchy, not to ensure nutritious food of all members of society. So, when a large amount of wealth is generated for some, it does not necessarily ensure nutritious food for all.

In the meritocracy, the objectives of the society are imposed by those who occupy the highest positions in the social hierarchy; and all the members of the society are forced to work for those objectives. Otherwise, they are alienated from the society, and are ruled over by the "deserving" and they might lose their social position, their food, home, and physical security. This means that there is no freedom for the members of society to choose the objectives of their society, or for them to choose their own goals and life projects. The goals of society are chosen by the "merited" and the individual adopts them or suffers the consequences.

Meritocracy can be one of the most effective forms of social organization to achieve its objectives. Because everyone in the structure is incentivized or conditioned to sacrifice their personal projects in favor of those of the meritocracy and dedicate as much time as possible to obtaining the necessary merits to move up the social hierarchy.

Do you think that because a person spends more time than you to generate more money or move up the social hierarchy, they have the right to choose the objectives of your society and the goals of your life? Do you think that because a person obtained more opportunities at the beginning of his life that gave him a competitive advantage, he should have power over you? According to your criteria, is a person "better" for spending more time at work generating money and less time in their social, family, personal, intellectual, or artistic life? Do you want to be ruled by those who reject everything in their life except climbing the hierarchy of meritocracy? Do we really consider it wise, good, and fair to empower people who dedicate their entire lives to achieving the merits of the system and rejecting their other goals in life? Do you think that those who dedicated their whole lives to climbing the social hierarchy should make the decisions that affect you, your life, and your circumstances?

Do you still have doubts about the systems of government that give power to a few over the many? Do you think it convenient that few decide the objectives of all? Is it convenient for few to decide what everyone can do, everyone's freedoms, opportunities, and possibilities? Is it just and convenient that a few people determine or influence the circumstances that affect and influence your development, your life, the life of all human beings and all living beings on the planet? Do you think it is convenient that a few people should have all the power in a society? If your answer is yes, please write your justification and email it to me so that I can respond directly to your arguments. Perhaps we can both learn from this debate.
objectivecracy@gmail.com or wejustcoop@gmail.com

CHAPTER 7

Democracy

The government of the people

We return to the concept we started with, democracy. Before continuing let us remember why electoral representative democracy is not a system that is convenient for us, and why we should strive to change the system.

The system of electoral representative democracy is not a truly democratic system. It concentrates power in a few hands, it polarizes and divides society, it is inefficient and very easily corrupted, because:

1) The candidate who wins the elections does not represent all citizens, he is only supposed to represent those who voted for him, so he can ignore, work against interests, and oppress those who did not vote for him.

2) Candidates and political parties often polarize society and, by doing so, they destroy the social fabric; by demonizing and condemning the opposition and those who vote for the opposition, they turn citizens against each other generating enemies out of people with different ideas. Political parties and politicians are stimulated by the system to portray their rivals as "opressores" or the "enemy" of their electorate, and by doing so, they polarize and divide the society.

3) Candidates and political parties don't have to represent their electorate in a positive way, they do not have to work for the things their electorate wants, they only have to convince their electorate to vote for them to protect themselves from the opposition, which they have demonized.

4) It is impossible for an elected representative to represent every single person that voted for him on every issue. A representative can represent a person on one issue and legislate or act against his interest on many other issues. Even the best-intentioned representatives cannot represent everyone that voted for him on every single issue.

5) Representatives often balance their own interests with those of their political parties, the groups that allow and help them to be in power, and the interests of the people who voted for them. It is a system in which one person represents himself, his political party, the powerful groups that help him obtain power, and his electorate.

6) The system gives a lot of power to the elected representatives, but they are limited human beings, and one mistake of theirs will affect the entire society they rule over.

7) During an election, citizens are forced to choose among the options presented to them by the political parties. This implies that the citizen can only choose from the options some other people chose for them. So not all citizens have the same power within a system of electoral representative democracy. The people who vote in the political parties' primaries and who finance the political campaigns decide who the candidates will be. The rest of the citizens can only choose from the options that are given to them.

8) The system of representative democracy by election is a highly inefficient one as each elected government can eliminate the progress made by the past administration. There is no defined goal for the whole of society and the political apparatus to strive for.

9) The electoral representative democracy system is highly inefficient because it encourages governments and representatives to work for short-term results that attract the attention of their electorate, and not to achieve the best long-term results.

10) The separation of powers, advisable to stop tyranny, may also render the representatives of a locality unable to work for the interests and objectives of their constituents.

11) Once a government is elected, some, or all, citizens lose their right to participate and their power. For there to be representatives, the represented must be absent. It is a system in which the representatives have all the power to govern and the represented have no power and are governed.

12) Democracy is government by the people not by the politicians elected by some of the people.

Some critics of democracy claim that democracy has failed, when in reality what has failed is electoral representative democracy, which in reality is not a democratic system. It is a system with which we can find countless problems even in theory. It is not that the system has failed because it has been democratic, it is because the system has never been democratic that it has failed. The problems generated by the lack of democracy in an "electoral representative democracy" are not solved by returning to less democratic systems, where the power of the few over the many is enlarged, where exploitation and oppression are facilitated and justified. The solution to the problems we face lies in more and more efficient democratic systems, not in more authoritarian systems.

Democratic systems are the only ones that aspire to protect every human being from oppression and to potentiate and expand the freedoms, possibilities, and opportunities of all members of society equally. Only a democratic system aspires to protect those who have less power from those who have more power. This does not mean that all democratic systems succeed in doing so, but that only a democratic system has the aspiration to protect all its members from oppression and to enhance the freedoms, possibilities, and opportunities of all members of society.

Only a democratic system strives to give the opportunity to all members of society to decide, influence, or determine the circumstances in which they live, develop, and which they face. This does not mean that all democratic systems allow it or achieve it equally, but that only democratic systems strive to give each citizen the opportunity to influence the circumstances in which he lives.

Only a democratic system allows members of society to decide what freedoms they are going to give up, what power they are going to restrict, what are the responsibilities and duties of each person, and what they have to do to belong to the society. Only a democracy allows members of society to participate in the decision-making process that determines what benefits society will give its members, what will be the goals and projects society will strive for, and how will the collective actions of the society impact the environment and the circumstances in which each member of society develops and lives.

Only a democratic system allows citizens to choose or decide the objectives of their society. Only a democratic system allows the possibility for a society, a nation, or a state, to be a common project for all its citizens. It is only through democracy that society becomes a common and personal project for all citizens.

Have you decided to be a free human being that lives and develops in a free society and that influences or determines the circumstances in which you develop? Do you think it is possible to live in a true democracy? Do you think it is possible for you to participate in making decisions that will impact and affect you? Do you want to be part of a free society where you can collaborate with other free human beings to generate the circumstances, opportunities, and possibilities that everyone wants to have? Do you want others to have the power to oppress you? Do you yourself want the power to oppress others or do you want to belong to a society without oppression?

____

____

____

____

____

____

____

____

____

____

True democracies

If you have decided to be free, if you have decided that you want to take control of your life, to be part of the decision-making process, to decide and influence the world in which you live and in which you develop, if you have decided to not oppress others, if you have decided that you want to be a free person among free people, the next step is to search and look for a social organization system that allows you to do so. We know that this system has to be democratic, but what would this democracy be like? How would it work? How would this society organize itself to be truly democratic?

There are already some proposals for democratic systems that do not have the problems and vices of the electoral representative system. Some have other problems, some may not be efficient, but we must consider them all; we must consider all possibilities, even the combination of different systems, to make them more efficient, more just, more democratic and stable. In the next pages, we are going to analyze different democratic systems that already exist and after that I am going to propose a new system of democratic social organization that I think is more efficient, more democratic, just, and more participatory than the others. But the idea of this book and its proposal is not about having a single answer, imposing one system on others ... that would not be very democratic, would it?

The objective we have right now is to use our capacity for abstraction, our reasoning, our creativity, our knowledge, and experiences to think about the best way in which we can organize ourselves in free societies. We do not have to arrive at a single answer, or a single system; there can be several. One system may work for one community, another for another one. A town of less than 10,000 inhabitants may decide that there is a type of democracy that works for them. A city of 1.5 or 20 million may need a different system, a country might choose another one.

It is important to consider how all these societies will interact with each other, but it is not necessary that they all be organized in the same way. The objective we set for ourselves is not to homogenize, it is to allow freedom, it is to increase the possibilities and opportunities of all human beings through the creation of free societies, of free human beings who cooperate with each other to achieve their common objectives; not the restriction, not the submission, not the homogenization and the elimination of the differences, but the celebration of the differences, the defense of the individuality of each human being, of each society, and the free collaboration between individual human beings and different societies to generate more opportunities, possibilities, and freedoms for all.

"We want a world where many worlds fit". EZLN [5]

Now we will analyze other and older proposals for democratic systems. Evaluate them, think about what you like and what convinces you. If you think you would like to live in a society organized into one of these systems, take the banner of this system, get organized, talk to people, discuss the system, and find ways in which you can change the current system to that system that convinced you.

Direct Democracy

Direct democracy is a system under which each member of society chooses and votes for himself on all public affairs. In this system, there are no representatives, each citizen elects and votes and has the right to propose actions and laws. Each citizen votes, not for a representative, but for each law, and for each issue that will affect the entire society, each citizen has the ability to propose laws or corrections to laws.

This type of democracy solves almost all the problems of representative democracy. Having no representatives, direct democracy does not have the problem of representatives dividing and polarizing the population with inflammatory rhetoric; of representatives abusing their position to gain more political, military, or economic power; of representatives representing themselves, their party, and the powerful groups that keep them in office; of the generation of a political class that turns into an oligarchy; and the problem of the representatives of a sector of the population completely excluding the interests and oppressing the sector of the population that did not vote for them. Direct democracy removes the intermediary between the decision and the citizen. Direct democracy is a system in which citizens really have control of their society; in which citizens decide and influence the circumstances where they live, develop, and face.

Within direct democracies there are two types of systems that are worth separating.

Direct Democracy by Simple Majority

Direct democracy by simple majority is the system by which a majority of votes is sufficient to approve a law that will govern all members of society.

Against direct democracy by a simple majority, we can argue that a "de facto" majority dictatorship is generated over the minority. That is, the members of society who lose the vote have to accept the laws imposed by the majority of which they do not approve. This means that although everyone voted, some members of society will be governed by the decisions of other members of society.

In a direct democracy by simple majority, if the society has 10 million people, and 6 of them decide a law, the other 4 million will have to accept that which was decided by the 6 million people. If the 4 million people consider that the decision of the other 6 million people is oppressive or contrary to their interests, the society will be polarized and divided, because there is no middle ground or consensus among all members of society. This is a system that will generally generate binary proposals with "yes" and "no" answers.

In a direct democracy by simple majority, it is not necessary for all citizens to reach an agreement, instead a group of citizens wins over others and imposes the law that will influence and determine the circumstances in which all citizens will live. Just as in an electoral representative democracy, this system will always generate winners and losers, the loser might feel or in fact be oppressed, and this will tend to polarize the society. This is a system in which the majority rules over the minorities. This could seem to be a natural consequence of a voting system or an inevitable consequence of a democracy, but it is not. There are democratic systems in which the majority cannot impose its absolute will on the minority.

We should also consider that the nations that we currently have are of hundreds of thousands, millions, or hundreds of millions of people, so it is safe to assume that if societies composed of this number people were to organize themselves through direct democracy by simple majority, the decisions taken by everyone will disproportionately affect some members of the population. Some people will be immediately and negatively affected by decisions taken by people who are not affected by the decision or law. When a person is not affected, or at least is not immediately or visibly affected by a decision, many incentives to learn, be informed, and consciously deliberate on the issues and their consequences, are eliminated. It is natural to assume that when people do not perceive how a decision will affect them, they will not have the interest to study the issue, deliberate, debate, and consider different opinions. This system will incentivize citizens to make decisions that can negatively affect others, and maybe themselves, in ways that they are not aware of, without investigating and deliberating.

Since all citizens vote for everything, all the time, no citizen is truly responsible, and no one can be held accountable for the negative consequences of a bad decision. When all citizens decide in a particular situation and the consequences are not the desired ones, no one can be held responsible for that decision and its consequences.

Since citizens are not held accountable for their decisions, they are not incentivized to analyze, debate, and deliberate, because they do not have, or feel, responsibility for the results, especially if they or the majority do not suffer the negative consequences of their decisions immediately. This system incentivizes people to not feel responsible for their decisions and their consequences.

In a direct democracy all citizens are expected to vote for absolutely all public issues. However, it is to be expected that even if all the citizens make the effort to inform themselves, they cannot know about every public issue, and they cannot be experts on everything. Therefore they will usually vote and decide without the proper knowledge to make a decision that will have the result they desire.

We should also consider that if the members of a society do not have a clear and common objective, their decisions will be erratic and there will be no objective measure to judge the results of the decisions. One day they will make a decision that will push society in one direction and another day they will make another decision that will push them in another direction and there will be no clear measures to evaluate the results of the decisions.

Furthermore, this system is not efficient since the members of the society would have to be involved in absolutely every decision and public affair. This requires a large amount of time on the part of citizens just to know the proposals and vote, not to mention the time necessary for each citizen to get informed and deliberate on each issue they have to decide on. It is a type of system in which a society's objective is not established, so the decisions and actions of the society will tend to be reactionary, focused on solving the immediate problems that citizens face when confronted with so many decisions. Having no real responsibility for the results, having a really small individual impact, and having other concerns in their life, they will hardly have the time, energy, and incentives to inform themselves and deliberate on all the issues they have to decide on.

However, we do need to acknowledge that this is a system in which every single citizen has the same amount of power. It is a system in which power is equally distributed among all citizens. The problem here is not in the distribution of power, as it is with all the other systems we have considered so far, the problem here is one of efficiency and of incentives. This is a system in which power is equally distributed among all citizens, but that can generate a dictatorship of the minorities over the minorities. Furthermore, citizens are incentivized to make decisions without the proper knowledge and deliberative process. They are overwhelmed by all the decisions they constantly have to make, and their decisions will tend to be reactionary and not positive and constructive.

Do you think that direct democracy by simple majority is better than electoral representative democracy? Do you think that direct democracy by simple majority is better than the systems of government in which the few govern the many? Can you think of examples and reasons why you do or don't like direct democracy by simple majority?

Direct Democracy by Consensus

Direct democracy by consensus is a system that seeks to generate a consensus among all members of society. In this system, it is not a majority that is necessary to make a decision, but, even if the majority wants something, if a minority is opposed, then the majority cannot impose a decision and must reach an agreement with the minority; a satisfactory agreement for absolutely all members of society. These agreements usually require a process of deliberation and debate in which different points of view are expressed and negotiated among all members of society to reach a consensus.

Direct democracy by consensus solves many of the problems of electoral representative democracy and the problem of mass dictatorship presented by direct democracy by simple majority. However, it cannot be expected that in absolutely all cases a consensus or agreement can be reached and, in this system, minorities will always have a much greater weight than the majority, because they can block any decision they disapprove of. The consequence of this is that minorities have more actual power because they can block the majority's proposals and they can stop laws and actions most members of society want to implement. The minority cannot pass its laws and rule over the majority, but the majority cannot pass a law that benefits the majority without the approval of the minority. This is something that protects all members of society, but it is also something that disproportionately benefits the minorities and tends to perpetuate inaction. In this system, it is easier for a resolution not to be approved than for it to be approved. This system favors the perpetuation of the status quo.

For example: If too much economic inequality is generated and 1% of the population holds all the economic power, this society will not be able to make changes to its tax laws to make the 1% pay more taxes if the 1% disagrees. A consensus would have to be reached between what the 1% want and what the 99% want.

Having made the above criticism, it should be emphasized that direct democracy by consensus is, of the types of social organization that we have analyzed so far, the one most protects individuals and that most encourages social participation, interaction, debate, and deliberation because to achieve a consensus, all sectors of society must meet, interact, present their points of view, their arguments, and negotiate with the other members of society.

However, the biggest problem of direct democracy by consensus is the size of the societies it can properly work on, and the type of projects that can be developed through a functioning direct democracy by consensus.

Currently, we have the ability to develop technology that can give all citizens the opportunity to vote all the time for absolutely all issues that affect their society. However, if the society is very large, one hundred thousand, one million, one hundred million people, etc. it will be difficult, if not impossible, to achieve a consensus among all citizens, so in practice it would be impossible to implement a consensus system for very large societies. In large societies, where citizens hold multiple opposing and irreconcilable opinions and desires, it is effectively impossible for every member of the society to reach a consensus. Furthermore, in large societies, the process of negotiation among all individual members of the society will be practically impossible to organize. This problem of direct democracy by consensus is one that direct democracy by simple majority does not have.

For a direct democracy by consensus to work, for negotiations to take place in which all members of the society participate, and in order for them to reach a consensus, the society must be small. Direct democracy by consensus can work perfectly in small societies, especially if the majority of the people in these societies have similarities in education and goals. However, a small society governed by direct democracy by consensus will hardly have the ability to generate large scale objectives and projects. In a completely connected world like the one we live in today, it is necessary to have a system of social organization that can organize small and large societies, that can undertake small and large-scale projects and that can face the problems and situations that affect millions of people, hundreds of millions, and even the entire planet.

For direct democracy by consensus to work, today's society would have to be divided into small units in which members can meet, debate, deliberate, negotiate, and reach a common consensus. But if the current societies are divided into such small units so as to make direct democracy by consensus possible, the result will be a system in which the small societies will hardly be able to form societies among themselves to face and solve large-scale problems or to undertake large-scale projects that would benefit all. If a small community reaches a consensus and wishes to interact with another community, how can they reach a consensus between the two communities or between 5, 10, or 1,000 other communities? If between the communities there is a direct democracy by consensus, that implies that absolutely all the members of each society unite to deliberate, debate, negotiate, and reach a consensus, a process that will be practically impossible when hundreds, thousands, hundreds of thousands, millions, or billions of people are involved. If each small community sends a delegate to negotiate with the other societies, then a representative system would be created with all the problems that this entails.

Perhaps right now you are wondering why it is necessary to generate interactions and societies among societies? Wouldn't it be better for humanity to limit itself to organizing in small scale societies?

1. The problems we are facing right now are monumental and global in scale.

1.   2. Restricting collaboration among communities limits the freedoms and the opportunities that are created by the collaboration of human beings.

Some of the problems that we humans face right now are not specific to a small society and will not be solved by limiting cooperation between societies and people. Problems like pandemics, diseases that affect all humans such as cancer and AIDS, droughts in a region that cause famines, extreme poverty, the climate crisis, etc. are not going to be solved by isolating human beings in small communities.

If there is no way to democratically organize many small-scale societies so that they can interact and work together, then the apparent solution would seem to be to isolate every small society and to completely close each society to the outside world. This way they can have a functioning direct democracy by consensus and citizens would be free inside every small society. However, this isolation will make it impossible for societies and humans to collaborate to solve large scale problems and to undertake large-scale projects that generate more opportunities, possibilities, well-being, and freedoms for all human beings. Isolation might limit oppression by other human beings, and other societies, but it will also limit the opportunities, possibilities, and freedoms of all human beings.

Furthermore, one of the stated objectives of democracy is the freedom of the human being, and if, in order to have a functioning small scale democracy, people are prohibited from relating to people from other societies, then every single human being's freedom is being limited and constricted. Society itself, by prohibiting interactions and relations among societies and among the members of different societies, will be limiting the opportunities, possibilities, and freedoms of all its members; the freedom or opportunity to interact and relate with other human beings, to learn from them, to cooperate, compete, and undertake joint ventures. Isolating each community and prohibiting the interaction among members of different societies would be to limit all the possibilities, opportunities, and freedoms that the human being generates when he works together and interacts with other humans. It is by working together and interacting among all human beings that we are able to increase our possibilities and opportunities, that we are able to increase our freedoms through shared knowledge, through cooperation, through trade, through technology developed by some and enjoyed by all, and through joint projects that expand our opportunities and possibilities.

Direct democracy by consensus only works in small scale societies that do not interact and relate to each other. To do so would be to limit the freedoms, opportunities, and possibilities of the human being. If a society seeks to respect and enhance human freedoms and tries to do so through a system that limits its possibilities and opportunities, then that action goes against the desired objective. The freedom to interact and join efforts generates more opportunities and possibilities for everyone involved and therefore expands everyone's freedoms. The more human beings interact with each other, sharing knowledge, technology, resources, efforts, and experiences, the more opportunities, possibilities, and freedoms they generate. The opportunities, possibilities, and freedoms in a society are directly proportional to the number of people that freely interact among themselves.

Conclusions on direct democracy

Direct democracy by consensus is a system that limits oppression but it also favors inaction and it only works in very small societies. It is a system in which a minority can block the decisions and progress of the majority and it is not a system through which a large number of people can be organized.

Direct democracy by simple majority is a system that works in large societies but can generate the oppression of minorities by majorities where there will always be winners and losers and therefore a tendency to polarize society and in which the decision-making process will tend to be uninformed and without a prior deliberation process.

Furthermore, both systems require a lot of time and effort on the part of the members of each society, even if they do not specialize in each subject or are not interested in all subjects they will vote on.

Do you think that direct democracy by consensus is better than representative democracy by election or than direct democracy by simple majority? Can you think of an argument to defend direct democracy by consensus? Can you think of more criticism? What parts do you like about these systems? How big do you think a society would have to be for direct democracy by consensus to work?

Sortition Democracy

Sortition democracy or democracy by lottery is the oldest system of organized and institutionalized democracy that we know of. This type of democracy was the system that was used in Athens during its golden age. That's right, in Athens there was no voting for representatives, the representatives were selected by lottery. [6] In fact, it was a combined system, in which public officials elected by lottery organized and moderated the agendas of citizens' assemblies, where all citizens could participate to expose problems, propose solutions and vote through direct democracy by simple majority; the decisions made by the assemblies were executed by public officials chosen by lottery. Except for the generals, all public positions were filled by lottery and most of the decisions were approved or vetoed through direct democracy by simple majority in an assembly where all citizens could participate. Ancient Athens' democracy was a combination between direct democracy by simple majority and sortition democracy.

In fact, since ancient times, the distinction between lottery and elections was understood by thinkers and philosophers as the distinction between democracy and oligarchy:

"The appointment of magistrates by lot is thought to be democratic and the election of them oligarchic. " Aristotle 7

"The suffrage by lot is natural to democracy, as that by election is to aristocracy." Montesquieu 8

In its purest form, sortition democracy is a system in which there are public officials who act on behalf of citizens but, unlike electoral representative democracy, they are randomly chosen by lot from among the citizens. In this system there are no political parties, professional politicians, or votes for representatives; the ideal is to educate and train all citizens to fulfill public functions since any member of society can be selected by lottery to serve as a government official.

There are different ways in which the principle of democracy by lottery can be applied. Assemblies composed of citizens selected by lot can be set up where public affairs are deliberated and where resolutions are reached by consensus or simple majority. Assemblies can be set up for each area of government or for special matters. There are different ways in which a system can be developed that uses democracy by lottery but the basic principles are:

1) There are assemblies or committees that dedicate all their time and talent to learning, deliberating, debating, proposing, and deciding on issues that affect the lives of all citizens.

2) There are assemblies or committees that are dedicated to executing or implementing the actions and laws decided and approved.

3) There is not a single person who is the head of the government, all decisions and actions are made by committees or assemblies. In this way, power is distributed and the risk of corruption and abuse of power is reduced.

4) The members of these committees and these assemblies are selected by lottery among all the citizens. There are no votes for representatives, there are no politicians, there are no political parties. All public officials are randomly selected from among all the citizens.

5) Public positions are short-term and officials are held accountable.

Usually, the proposals of these types of systems detect the different demographics of society and choose a proportional number of representatives of each demographic by lottery. For example, if there are 50% women and 50% men in a society, the sortition process will be designed to select 50% of women for the assemblies. If there are 60% Christians, 30% Muslims, and 10% atheists in society, then they will be proportionally represented.

The advantages of this type of democracy are:

1) It eliminates the electoral process and the political campaigns in which the population is usually polarized. It eliminates some of the problems of the electoral representation systems and the possibility that a representative elected by the people will turn into a dictator. Dictators can, and tend to, emerge from electoral

representative democracies but not from sortition democracies.

2) It eliminates or reduces the possibility of powerful groups controlling candidates and representatives because these groups have no way of knowing in advance which candidate will be chosen by lot. This means that the possibility of generating oligarchies or aristocracies of the political class is eliminated.

3) It allows citizens' representatives to give their full time and attention to public affairs as they are made responsible for the results of the decisions they take. This eliminates some problems of direct democracy.

4) Although not all citizens are experts in all subjects, since the representatives dedicate all their time to public affairs and are responsible for the results of their decisions, these people are encouraged to inform themselves, deliberate, and participate in debates where different points of view are exposed, arguments are given, and they will need to negotiate to reach a consensus or a majority. These citizens are not experts in everything, but they have the time and incentives to consult the experts in each subject on which they have to make decisions.

5) It enables large societies of hundreds of thousands, millions, and hundreds of millions of people to form, and therefore allows society to undertake large-scale projects.

This system is undoubtedly a democratic system and undoubtedly corrects some of the deficiencies of direct democracy and other problems of electoral representative democracy. However, it is not a perfect system.

The most common objection to this type of system is that the representatives who have been chosen by lot are people who are not necessarily competent to make decisions on all aspects of the public life of a society. It is not possible that all the people who are selected by lottery to be part of the assemblies have the levels of knowledge and the critical and analytical capacity to make decisions in absolutely all the areas involved in a society. However, this problem also emerges in the election of representatives. Politicians are not experts on all the issues which they have to deliberate, and the solution in this case would be to give members of the assemblies teams of experts who advise them and allow them a period of immersion in the system and in the subjects on which they are going to deliberate, just as is done in current governments when a politician is moved from one office to another or a specific committee is opened within the chamber of legislators. Currently, all politicians hire teams to advise them and the same happens with members of the assembly elected by lottery. In fact, the members of an assembly elected by lottery will have more time to learn and deliberate than those who are elected by vote because in an electoral representative democracy, much of the representatives' time is spent working on their image to gain popularity, be re-elected, and to work for their personal interests, the interest of their political parties, and of the powerful groups that helped them obtain power. Representatives elected by lottery will not have to spend time on these partisan negotiations or seek resources or public attention to win reelection or other political office. Therefore, the representatives elected by lottery will have more time and energy than those elected by voting to dedicate to legislative and government work, without pressure from parties and powerful groups.

There are some proposals of systems of democracy by lottery that propose various legislative bodies with different powers that regulate and review each other to prevent legislation proposed by a group of incompetent or oppressive legislators from being approved. The problem of the incompetence of some is solved with the participation of many in different government bodies with different powers that regulate each other.

For example, one chamber of legislators elected by lottery determines the topics on which the next chamber of legislators who propose a law will work, another chamber evaluates the proposed law and presents its conclusions to a jury composed of citizens elected by lottery who decide whether this law is approved or not.

However, the problem of incompetence is not exclusive to this type of democracy, our current system, electoral representative democracy also presents the same problem. Incompetence is not solved by having been elected, incompetence to legislate is not eliminated by being the heir of a powerful family, incompetence to legislate is not eliminated by being a lawyer, a great businessman, an actor, or a famous comedian. The main reason for incompetence to legislate in a democratic society comes from lack of understanding, consideration, and empathy among the members of a society. From the lawyer to the farmer, from the employer to the worker, the comedian to the housewife, etc. This understanding of the situation that other people are experiencing, consideration for them and empathy towards their cause, is resolved when the legislative body is made up of citizens from all socioeconomic strata chosen by lot.

Other objections to the system are:

1) In most democratic by lottery system proposals, citizens are separated by demographics and within these demographics a representative is chosen by lottery. Demographics are often racial, economic, gender, or religious. A demography is a classification of characteristics that may have nothing to do with the positions in political and public affairs that a person may hold. In this case, demographic selection is a simplification of large numbers of people to a single categorization.

For example, a Latino may or may not be a Christian, he may be a Buddhist, he may be an atheist, he may be a Marxist, a capitalist or a socialist, he may be for or against abortion. The characteristic that places you within a demographic category does not determine your personal positions. It can predict some, but not all.

On the other hand, if the population is not separated by demographics, there is a risk that more people of one type or class will be chosen by chance than another, generating an imbalance of interests in the legislative and executive bodies of the government. If the population is not separated by specific and simplistic demographics, there is a risk that many more people from a single demography will be chosen by lot and therefore that their interests will be more represented than those of the rest of society.

2)   In large societies of hundreds of thousands of people, or millions, most citizens will never be selected to participate in these processes; so most of them will never participate, they will never be able to deliberate, they will never be able to choose. Their circumstances will be chosen by the citizens selected by lot, not by themselves.

Because it is also a representative system, democracy by lottery is not a participatory system. By not participating directly in decisions or indirectly through a representative of their choice, most citizens will not have any kind of participation in the decision-making process. By not choosing, citizens do not participate and may think, perceive, or feel that the laws are imposed on them by people they do not know, and that the laws have more to do with chance than with what members of society actually want. This can generate the perception that the objectives, terms, and conditions of their social contract and the circumstances in which they live are determined by chance and luck and not by free agreement among them and the rest of the citizens. For those who have not been chosen by lot to participate, there may be a feeling that external forces determine their circumstances and have power over them and not that they, the citizens, have the power themselves. This continues to be a representation system in which not everyone will be represented; and the fact that the government officials are chosen by lot might delegitimize some of their decisions, especially if they are unpopular.

3)   Citizens working in the legislative bodies will have an internal process; they will deliberate, debate, and have personal growth, which will lead them to reach certain conclusions that the citizen who is not involved and who does not undergo the same process may not understand. This lack of understanding of the conclusions reached by these randomly elected citizens can lead to

mistrust in the legislative process, especially if the results of a law are not very popular.

4) Sortition democracy is a representative system by chance, therefore unelected citizens will not have the slightest participation in choosing the objectives, terms, and conditions of their society. In large populations, it is to be expected that the vast majority of citizens will never be chosen by lot to be representatives, or they will be elected no more than once. This system will not allow all citizens to develop in the public sphere. They will not be governed by an aristocracy, an oligarch, or a dictator, but neither will they be a direct part of the democratic process. They will live in a democratic system, but most likely they will not participate in the democratic process. Therefore, the lottery system eliminates the problems of direct democracy but returns some problems of electoral representative democracy, the fact that most members of a society are not active participants in the democratic process and in the decision-making process that affects them.

What do you think of democracy by lottery? Do you think it could be a system that you can live under? Would you agree more with the decisions made by the citizens' assemblies chosen by lot than the decisions made by politicians? Do you think you could trust randomly selected citizens more than politicians? What do you like and dislike about this system?

____

____

____

____

____

____

____

____

____

____

Combination of Different Democratic Systems

Many of the objections and problems of democracy by lottery or direct democracy can be solved with a combination of both systems. As we said earlier, the first democracy, that of Athens in the 5th century BC, was a combination of democracy by lottery with direct democracy by simple majority. Citizens chosen by lottery organized the topics that would be discussed in the citizens' assemblies where around six or eight thousand citizens attended and anyone could debate, give their proposed solutions and legislations, and everyone voted by raising their hands. The decisions of the assembly were executed by a committee of citizens elected by lottery. Each year a new committee was elected and each committee member was responsible for the administration of the committee for only one month. This process ensured that all citizens had the opportunity to participate in the legislative process where the laws and actions of the entire city were discussed; it was ensured that those who executed the laws did not have too much power, were not members of an oligarchy, and could not be corrupted. Unfortunately, some of the problems of direct democracy continue to arise in the Athenian system, since in the assemblies a majority dictatorship is generated over the minority, and in societies of hundreds of thousands of members it would be impossible to generate assemblies where absolutely all citizens participate; therefore the Athenian system would hardly be applicable in modern societies.

However, the three democratic systems can be combined in different ways. Ideally they combine to solve the problems that emerge when applying only one type of democracy.

For example, a society can be developed where citizens' legislative assemblies are chosen by lot to deliberate and propose laws that they present to the public and all citizens vote to approve or veto this law. In this way by lottery, legislative chambers are generated where citizens inform themselves, debate, deliberate, and negotiate on public affairs, and when they reach a conclusion they propose it to citizens who, through the use of direct democracy, approve or reject the proposal.

This would be a combination of democracy by lottery and direct democracy by simple majority. Legislators are chosen by lot, and a law is approved or vetoed by a majority of the entire population.

The advantages of this system are that:

1. The people selected by lottery are not professional politicians, they are not part of a powerful interest group, they do not campaign, and they do not receive money from political parties, groups, or businessmen.

2. People selected by lottery dedicate their full time to public affairs so they have enough time to study the topics and problems about which they have to legislate.

3. The people selected by lottery have the responsibility and are held accountable for the results of their decisions, therefore they must be convinced that what they decide is the best course of action. This will incentivise them to debate, hear opposing ideas and arguments, deliberate, negotiate, and reach an agreement with most of the other members of the assembly. This would help to generate informed proposals that are not aligned or influenced by party interests or that favor the

powerful or interest groups and that can be accepted by the majority of the population.

4. By submitting the resolution to a public vote, it is ensured that all citizens participate in the democratic process and therefore that the laws have legitimacy and that the laws are not something chosen by others, but by the citizen himself.

The combination of these systems can generate a system that has legitimacy, that is truly democratic, that protects citizens from oppression and that is efficient. It is worth studying and thinking about what the best way to combine and apply these systems would be.

Until now, the combination of democratic systems solves the problems of electoral representative democracy, the problems of direct democracy by simple majority and by consensus, and some of the problems of democracy by lottery.

We could finish the book right now and start becoming activists for the combination of these democratic systems. However, I think we can manage to develop a better system, as there are still a couple of aspects that I think are not one hundred percent convincing about the systems resulting from the combination of democracy by lottery and direct democracy by majority. Now I will develop my arguments against the system resulting in the combination of these two types of democracy and it is for you to decide if you agree with me or if you are satisfied with the combination of these systems.

Objections

Some citizens, those chosen by lot, will participate intensively in the democratic process, setting the goals of society, the permitted, the prohibited, the stimulated, the discouraged, the freedoms, rights, obligations, and restrictions of all other citizens. Some citizens will be more involved than others in the construction of the world and the circumstances in which everyone will live. All may vote to accept or not the resolutions reached by the representatives selected by lottery, but their participation is minimal; their only participation is to accept or reject. This is better than not participating, but it is a very small amount of participation. I think that there may be a system in which everyone has the opportunity to participate much more, not just accepting or rejecting what the citizens' assemblies propose to them.

On the other hand, by asking all citizens to vote whether or not they want to approve a resolution, this system continues to have the problems of direct democracy. It still requires a monumental amount of time on the part of citizens to be able to make informed and deliberate decisions, time that not all citizens have, and even if they do, they may feel that their vote counts for very little alongside the other thousands or millions of votes; or they may even feel or think that they could propose something better than what the assemblies have; and that reducing their involvement to approve or veto is something more limiting than stimulating.

Furthermore, although it is a system in which citizens vote directly to approve the resolution, or not, proposed by the committees selected by lottery, it is not a system that encourages participation. It is a system that encourages passivity, in which most citizens will never participate intensively to choose the circumstances in which they will live. They only approve or veto.

The combination of the systems is more defensive than constructive. It is a system that protects and defends the individual, That protects the individual from those who have power and would use it to oppress him, That protects the individual from the oligarchies or tyrants; but it is not a system that builds, that invites its citizens not to defend themselves from the world, not to approve and disapprove, but to build and collaborate; to actively participate in building a world together with other citizens.

This is a system where few propose and everyone decides whether to accept or not, but it is not a system where everyone has the opportunity to build their own society; where society is not something accepted or denied but something in which we participate and build together. This is not a system that encourages participation. It is not a system that encourages all members of society to unite to build their own and common circumstances for all members of society. It is a democratic system, but not very participatory.

This is the best system we have discussed so far. It is a system worth considering. It may be the best system that we find, or the best system that we can evolve to in the short or medium term. Think about it and analyze it. I personally think that this is a great system, but that we can develop a better one. What do you think? What advantages do you think a system has where members of legislative assemblies are selected by lot and where all citizens vote directly to approve or reject all the proposals presented by these assemblies?

____
____
____
____
____
____
____
____
____
____
____
____
____
____
____
____

Even if the previous systems convince you, I ask you to continue reading, because from now on it only gets better. If you are already convinced by the combination of direct democracy with democracy by lottery, I recommend you search the internet for political parties and associations that seek to implement direct democracy or democracy by lottery in some countries. Maybe you can join an effort that is already underway, or maybe you can start a new one.

Remember that what I discuss in this book are only the basic principles of each system, and that there are many different ways to apply them. For example:

1. The Zapatistas in Mexico have a combination of direct democracy by consensus and majority rule.

2. The Kurds in Rojava have developed a system that combines direct and representative democracy.

3. In some Swiss villages, direct democracy is used to vote on local issues.

4. In the city of Porto Alegre, Brazil, citizens directly decide what the local budget will be invested in.

5. There are political parties that propose to inject direct democracy into the electoral representative democracy system in the USA, Canada, Brazil, Thailand, Israel, Japan, the Netherlands, Italy, Ireland, Croatia, Finland, Bulgaria, Germany, Spain, Portugal, Sweden, the United Kingdom, Poland, Australia, and New Zealand.

6. From 2000 to 2020, 120 citizen assemblies have been formed around the world, where members are chosen by lottery and present recommendations to their governments. Some of the most notorious of these are the citizens' assemblies formed in Ontario and Vancouver, Canada, to propose changes to the electoral law; and a constitutional convention in Ireland.

Regardless of the system that convinces you, I think that the first thing we have to do is recognize that electoral representative democracy is not democratic and that we have to find a new system. In a world where almost all human beings live oppressed in one way or another, I think the most important and urgent conversation at this moment is about how we are going to organize ourselves as a society so that we can be free and so that we can collaborate to expand our opportunities and possibilities, and face and solve the problems of inequality, the climate crisis, the pandemic, etc.

Analyze the following proposal, debate it, and let us fight together to be free and for the right to collaborate and to decide and build the world and circumstances in which we live.

SECTION 4

A NEW SYSTEM

CHAPTER 1

Analogy

Democracy is a means and end in itself.

We have the capacity to develop a democratic system that is a means and an end in itself. A means that allows us to live in society respecting each other and protecting us from the powerful and would be oppressors. An end in itself because through the democratic process we can participate, develop our human capacities, increase our opportunities, freedoms, and possibilities, increase the interaction with other members of the society to develop personal relationships with them, or to compete against them, to learn from them, to cooperate and build projects for our own or the whole society' sake.

Just like a house can be a means to protect a family from the elements and can be a home that permits and stimulates the family to develop their bonds and live happy existences, the democratic process can be a means to protect citizens from oppression and an end in itself, the circumstances in which a free person wants to live and in which he has more opportunities to develop.

Democracy does not have to be something far away from us, it can be the way in which we relate to other people, with other members of society, seeing in each of them an ally to develop the world and the circumstances in which we want to live, a possible ally to undertake a common project, a person with whom you can interact because you know you have common goals, a person with whom perhaps you are going to compete and discuss, but, by doing it democratically, the process of competing and discussing will lead you to learn and develop your skills even further. Living in a free democracy is also knowing that even the competitors, even your opponents, even those who think differently from you, respect you, your life, your freedom, and might even be working for the same goals as you are, and it is thanks to the union between them and you that you can be free and have so many opportunities. It is because you live in a free society that you have opportunities, possibilities, and freedoms that you would not have otherwise. It is thanks to the fact that you live in a free society that you can undertake large-scale projects that will have a transcendent impact for you, for other members of your society, and the planet. The free union between all is what protects your freedom and allows you to increase it.

Right now, we do not live in this free society. In order to experience real democracy, to be able to make the democratic process a life experience, which is part of the reason why we develop and belong to our society. We have to have a system that allows us the opportunities to constantly participate in the democratic process so that the result of the democratic process is unifying and not divisive. We need to develop a system that allows individuality, protects it, celebrates it, needs it, but also generates union and cooperation; a system and a process that allows us to be ourselves as individuals and to be part of the whole of society. A system in which the process of democracy is one of living, of building, of common and personal endeavors and cooperation, and not a process in which we just wait or participate in order to hold off oppression. The systems and processes of the democracy we want is one that gives us the opportunity and capacity to build the world and the circumstances in which we want to live and not just a mechanism to protect us from oppression. We want the process of democracy itself to be a life experience, to be part of what we consider the good life, part of our personal purposes, part of the world, part of the circumstances under which we want to live. We want our free society to generate more opportunities, possibilities, freedoms, more experiences, and more life for everyone involved. The democratic process can be a means to achieve our objectives, to develop societies, and to make an impact on our circumstances and at the same time it can be an end in itself that allows us to collaborate with other citizens and generate life experiences.

CHAPTER 2

Characteristics of the New System

1)   The new system must be truly democratic.

This means that it must be a system in which all members of society, regardless of their gender, race, religion, or socioeconomic position, have the same rights, the same values, the same opportunities, and the same power. They are all protected from oppression and everyone participates in the decision-making process that affects them.

2)   The new system must allow and encourage all individuals to participate to the best of their possibilities, abilities, and desires. At the same time, the system must protect the whole society from those that do not have or want to have the time or capacity to investigate, deliberate, make decisions, and undertake projects that could negatively affect all other members of the society.

One of the problems with direct democracy is that it requires that all individuals be experts in everything and that they dedicate a large amount of time and effort to being informed and to making decisions, because if they do not do so, their decisions may be ignorant and have devastating consequences for all members of the society.

The problem of direct democracy is solved by representative democracy by lottery because it allows some people to dedicate all their time and energy to deliberate and debate on the issues on which they have to decide or act, and therefore they make informed and conscious decisions. The problem with the lottery system is that it does not encourage or allow all citizens to participate.

The new system must allow and encourage the participation of all citizens to the degree that they wish to get involved, but it must respect the private and personal time of each citizen, and the freedom that each citizen has to do with their time and energy what they want. Furthermore, the system must protect individuals and the society as a whole from the decisions of uninformed or disinterested individuals.

This means that all individuals within the system can participate, have the same rights and possibilities to participate, but that they are not obliged to dedicate all their time to public affairs and that an uninformed or incompetent decision or action of one should not have massively negative repercussions for everyone else.

The system must also encourage and allow individuals to participate in public, social, and community actions and projects that are of personal interest to them or in which they are experts and knowledgeable. The system must encourage each citizen to get involved as deeply as they want to get involved and in the issues with which they want to get involved. The system should incentivize and reward participation, but it should not overload citizens with matters they do not want to participate in. Participation should be incentivized, but it should remain a choice.

3)   The system must ensure that the participation of one individual is never oppressive to another individual or the society as a whole. The system must encourage individuals to participate and generate social cohesion through participation.

One of the problems for direct democracies by simple majority and electoral representative democracies is that they tend to polarize and divide the society. They are systems that will always generate winners and losers and the losers can be oppressed. This problem does not exist in direct democracy by consensus because it requires all members of a society to reach an agreement. The problem with this system is that it tends to inaction, it favors minorities, it only works with very small societies, and it requires a lot of time from each person involved for deliberation and negotiation.

The new system must generate social cohesion without generating losers, without oppressors and oppressed, and at the same time encourage action. As much as possible, effort should be made to avoid generating winners and losers, dictatorships of the majority or the minorities, and to avoid generating rulers and governed people. The new system must generate social cohesion, not polarization.

4) The new system must allow and celebrate individuality and differences within society, but it should find a way to generate social cohesion and union.

The system of representation by lottery and elections unites large numbers of people under a single representative, and treats them as if they were all one entity or as if a specific characteristic of the members of each demography defined their personhood completely.

The new system must allow each individual to be himself. Society exists for citizens, citizens do not exist for society. Each citizen is a unique human being, with similarities and differences with all other human beings. Each human being can be considered 100% individual and, at the same time, participate and be part of the group, of society.

The new social system must allow citizens to participate individually, not to be grouped into categories that simplify them, and that represent them in some things and not in others. The new system must allow each member of society to recognize part of his personal interests in the interests of the entire society and, at the same time, understand himself as an individual.

Naturally, if citizens are individuals and are not homogenized under one party, ideology, or demography, they will have opposing and irreconcilable ideas, interests, and objectives, this will generate antagonism inside the society. These differences and antagonisms are used by today's politicians to divide the entirety of the population into enemy groups. They communicate to the population that one or some differences they have with the other group of citizens are so fundamental that the members of the other group are their enemies in absolutely every single thing. The new system must consider, permit, and promote antagonisms as part of the democratic process, however it must focus each antagonism to the specific theme or idea where it exists and should not permit it to extend to other areas of public life. The system must allow people to diverge, to be different from one another, to oppose one another, or to compete with one another, but at the same time it must always show them that they have common ideas, interests and objectives with one another. It must permit and foment individual differences, but it must also show them where they converge and what they have in common even with those they oppose in some things. The system must not strive to homogenize its citizens. It should atomize all public affairs in such a way that every citizen will find in the other a person with some common ideas and objectives for their society and some other opposing, antagonistic, or competing ideas, objectives, or social projects. The system must foment in its citizens the realization that they have things in common and differences with almost every other human being, and that they can compete or oppose each other in their differences and can unite and collaborate through their similarities. This way, the system will be able to protect and foment individuality and social cohesion.

5)   The new system must allow, encourage, remunerate, and celebrate the participation of all citizens.

The representative democracy system, by lottery or election, excludes the majority of citizens from the political processes. The direct democracy system, by majority or by consensus, overwhelms citizens with issues on which they are not informed, decisions that matter little to them, or that affect them very much but that they might not know how to take a position on them. The new system should encourage citizen participation and, at the same time, give them the opportunity to choose how they participate and to what extent.

In the new system, participating is not only a right, but an opportunity to build the world you want for yourself and your society and to influence your circumstances. The new system should allow and encourage citizens to participate in the sectors of the public life in which they want to participate and in which they have the most knowledge and should reward them for their participation.

6) The new system must protect individuals and society itself from oppression by powerful individuals and groups.

In electoral representative democracy, elected officials often work for their personal interests, the interests of their political parties, or of their powerful allies and against the interests of a sector of the population. The new system must protect all members of society from those with enough power to oppress. The new system must be organized in such a way that will make it very difficult for a group to use its power to take control of the government, or impose decisions and oppress a sector of the population. It must be a system in which power is distributed among all citizens, and in which the concentration of power in a few hands is avoided.

7)   The new system has to protect individuals from the
     system itself and from the possibilities and
     opportunities to abuse power that the system itself
     generates.

Certain social structures can become oppressive. Perhaps the people
within the system do not want to be oppressive, but the structure itself
can be oppressive. The new system has to protect citizens from the
power that can accumulate in the system itself and that can be used
against the citizen. The new system has to be flexible and able to
evolve because rigid systems in an ever-changing world tend to
become oppressive.

8)   The new system should seek to limit and eliminate
     power and oppression while increasing cooperation.

The new system must allow, encourage, and generate collaboration
and the union of large numbers of people to undertake large-scale
personal and social projects, while limiting and eliminating power
and oppression. The new system must eliminate oppression and
generate more collaboration.

9)   The new system has to be very difficult, if possible
     impossible, to corrupt.

One of the arguments against change, any change, is that all systems
may seem perfect in theory, but when they are applied, they are
corrupted. The new system that we are going to develop must be very
difficult, practically impossible, to completely corrupt. The new
system, in its theory must be protected from possible forms of
corruption. The new system should seek to have mechanisms to
eliminate corruption and even mechanisms so that, if corruption

exists in a sector of the system, this corruption cannot be extended to the entire system and remains focalized and limited in scope.

10) There has to be clear accountability in the new system.

One of the problems with direct democracy by majority is that everyone votes for everything, so no one is really responsible for the consequences of decisions. One of the problems of democracy by lottery is that there are no clear objectives against which to measure the success of the decisions and actions of the representatives or citizen assemblies.

The new system should be one in which the results of public actions can be calculated and measured and in which accountability can be demanded, and the results of laws and actions executed by those responsible for carrying them out in the public interest be judged as objectively as possible.

11) The new system has to be able to evolve and at the same time it should always generate stability.

Morals, justice, and laws change and evolve over time, with the new experiences that individuals and societies experience, the new information they learn, the new points of view they develop, and the new philosophies that emerge. A rigid system that does not allow the evolution of society is a system that ends up being oppressive to its members, that does not allow them to open new horizons, remove chains and self-imposed limitations, or limitations imposed by previous generations, and build new worlds, new circumstances, create new possibilities and opportunities, and expand the freedoms of its members.

However, a system and a society that is always changing runs the risk of being inconsistent and unstable. If a society is unstable, then it is difficult to build a future and undertake large-scale and high-impact projects. The members of an unstable society, instead of finding security in their society, will find instability and insecurity. They will not be able to make plans for the future because they will not be able to predict in what circumstances they will find themselves in the future. A society requires sufficient consistency and continuity to allow individuals and society to plan for the long term and to build in the present the circumstances and the world in which they want to live in the future. However, the future cannot be static, it must be able to evolve to new futures, otherwise it becomes a ballast that closes possibilities.

The new society must be able to generate long-term stability and at the same time it must be flexible and evolve according to the individual evolution of the members of the society.

12) The new system must allow the undertaking of large-scale and high-impact projects.

The world right now is facing gigantic problems like the climate crisis, extreme poverty, and pandemics and diseases that afflict billions of people around the world. Isolating in small communities will not solve global problems, nor community problems. When human beings work together, we open up possibilities and create projects that would be impossible if we were isolated.

The new system must allow large-scale projects to be undertaken involving thousands, and even millions, of people. Projects that allow us to reverse climate change, protect endangered species worldwide, eradicate poverty and famine, find the cure for diseases, reduce inequality, eliminate the oppression of marginalized communities, develop infrastructure, new technologies, art, culture, shared experiences and life. All this will increase the possibilities, opportunities, and freedoms of the human being, protect the life of the human being and promote their personal and social development.

When united, human beings can do more than when alone. Together we can expand our freedoms, opportunities, and possibilities and be formidable when facing the problems that afflict us.

13) **The new system should be able to be applied in small communities and in large nations and it should allow democratic interaction among many societies.**

The system must be applicable regardless of the size of the community and it must be able to function properly and democratically when a society among different societies is created. The new system must allow collaboration among many different societies.

One of the problems with direct democracy by consensus is that it only works in small communities. It is illogical to think that in societies composed of hundreds, thousands, or millions, people will be able to reach a consensus on every issue. One of the problems of direct democracy by majority is that the larger the society, the less impact each individual has, and the less knowledge each individual will have of the issues that affect sectors of society of which they are not aware, or with which they are not directly related.

The new system must be able to function on a small and large scale; it must be able to form societies among different societies; it must be able to work for a neighborhood, for a town, for a city, for a country, for a continent, for the whole world.

A society organized under the new system must be able to interact and collaborate with other societies, or scale up without restricting the individual freedoms and the democratic characteristics of the system. It must be an effective system that is able to generate democratic collaboration among different societies in order to build a global organization. It should be able to interact and cooperate with societies that are organized through other systems or have replicated this same system and it is used by absolutely all societies in the world. This means that if a society manages to have the new system, it can organize itself democratically, legitimately, and efficiently with other societies that use the same or different systems.

If all the societies of the world use this new system, the different societies should be able to relate and collaborate with each other in a democratic way, respecting and stimulating the development of each society and of each individual within each society. The ideal is to be able to develop a system replicable to all human societies that allows them to have a democracy at the local level and at the same time that allows them to participate in a regional and even global democracy. Free individuals collaborating freely to develop a free local society, free local societies that collaborate freely to develop free regional societies, and free regional societies that collaborate freely in order to generate a free global society composed of free individuals that expand their possibilities, opportunities, and freedoms through free global collaboration.

Can you think of any other characteristics that you would like the new social system to have?

____

____

____

____

____

____

____

____

____

____

____

____

____

____

____

Now we are ready to develop, propose, and analyze the new system.

CHAPTER 3

Objectivecracy

Government by objectives.

To consciously develop a social contract, the first step is to determine the objectives of the social contract. Once the objectives are established, the terms and conditions to achieve the objectives are developed. Objectivecracy is the social organization system that centers the attention of the citizens on the objectives of the social contract. From these objectives, the citizens will develop the terms and conditions of the social contract and the laws, projects, and actions to achieve their objectives.

Objectivecracy is a system which organizes society to achieve a set of objectives. This means that there is no one person (king, president, prime minister, or dictator), nor a group of people (legislators, senators, aristocrats, or any form of oligarchy) who govern people. Rather, it is a list of objectives that dictate the public life of the members of society. The first step in this social system is to determine the objectives of society and from these objectives everything else follows. First, you decide which are to be the objectives of society and then you decide how to achieve them. Laws, public expenditures, public projects, the actions and the social structure, and the people who organize society must be aligned to achieve the objectives of the society. All public activity is designed to achieve the objectives of society and is evaluated according to how efficient they are in achieving these objectives.

The method of selecting the objectives and the way in which they will be sought may vary among societies and generate different systems. Just as the concept of democracy might be applied in different ways, such as in direct democracy and democracy by lottery, there are different ways in which the concept of Objectivecracy can be applied. The most important thing about Objectivecracy is that the social structure is designed to achieve certain objectives. The laws, the terms and conditions of the social contract, and the actions and projects that society will undertake together will be generated from and meant to achieve the society's objectives. The objectives of a society and the effort to achieve them will generate the circumstances in which the citizens live.

What does the Objectivecracy intend?

The first thing the Objectivecracy seeks is to establish common objectives for the whole of society. It establishes a list of objectives, ordered by priorities, that society strives to achieve through all public and common actions, decisions, and projects.

These objectives become the metrics and criteria through which all public action will be judged. Any law, expense, or public action will be judged according to the objectives of the society. It is the objectives that set the agenda and govern the society.

This means that the results of the laws, projects, or actions carried out by the society will have to be developed to achieve a specific objective and their result will be judged according to the objective sought. If there are clear objectives and goals, the results and consequences of laws, actions, and projects can be objectively evaluated and measured against the objectives of the society.

Why govern ourselves through a scale of objectives organized by priorities?

Having a clear set of objectives allows the members of society to know exactly why the society exists, what it is training to achieve, the circumstances it strives to generate, and have clear metrics to evaluate and judge all public decisions and actions.

To achieve the society's objectives, large-scale, high-impact social projects can be developed in which large parts of the population can work and collaborate. The projects, actions, and the laws of the society are not the objectives in themselves, but the means to achieve the objectives of the society. Once the objectives of the society are established, large or small actions and projects can be undertaken to achieve these goals. The laws and projects are developed to achieve an objective and are evaluated and judged according to the objective. If a law has consequences contrary to the objective, the objective remains but the law is changed. The law is there to achieve an objective and is judged according to how much it helps society achieve its goals.

By having a clear and visible list of objectives scaled by priorities, all members of society are aware of the objectives of their society; all members of society know what their society wants to achieve and the circumstances they want to create through their actions; and all members of society can objectively evaluate and judge the results of public and social decisions and actions.

What are the society's objectives?

An objective is something that is sought. In a society, the objectives are the circumstances in which the citizens want to live, and the benefits, opportunities, possibilities, and freedoms they want to generate together. In a society, an objective is the end sought by the social actions, and if it is achieved it will generate specific and desired circumstances or benefits for all the members of the society. The objective is not a specific action but the desired outcome of such action.

For example: an objective can be the equitable economic development of all the members of the society. To reach this objective, the citizens can develop many different laws, programs, and projects and their results will be evaluated and judged according to how effective and efficient they were in achieving the society's objectives. If a law, project, or action does not bring society closer to its objectives, it is revoked and replaced, but the objective remains.

The objectives of a society are the circumstances, benefits, opportunities, possibilities, and freedoms the society aspires to generate for its members. The organization and effort of the society to achieve the objectives will generate the terms and conditions, projects, and actions of the whole of society and all these together will generate the circumstances that the society wants for its citizens. The opportunities, possibilities, freedoms, benefits, duties, rights, restrictions, and limitations to freedoms and power are all a consequence of striving to achieve an objective.

Types of Objectivecracy

The particular way in which the Objectivecracy is applied will determine if it is democratic, plural, and if it promotes freedom and human development or if it is a homogenizing and oppressive system. The general concept of Objectivecracy is so neutral that it can be applied to institute a type of dictatorship that enforces the preservation of certain values and objectives, or a democratic society in which ideas and objectives are freely discussed and decided by all members of society. From now on, I propose a specific type of Objectivecracy: Democratic Objectivecracy.

CHAPTER 4

Democratic Objectivecracy

In its simplest form, without a particular application (since even the concept of Democratic Objectivecracy can be applied in many different ways), the Democratic Objectivecracy is a system in which the members of a society democratically choose the objectives of their society. The objectives from which all the actions and laws of the society will be derived over a specific period of time.

The first thing to understand about the Democratic Objectivecracy is that members of society democratically choose the objectives for which they will strive together; the reason why they want to be united as a society. These objectives may be the circumstances in which every individual wants to live; the benefits, opportunities, possibilities, and freedoms they want their society to give them; the world they wish to develop and build for themselves and for all members of society.

By choosing the objectives of their society, citizens choose their reason for being part of the society and what they expect and want from their society.

There are many, many ways in which a Democratic Objectivecracy can be organized; many, many ways in which these societal objectives can be chosen; and many ways in which society can be organized to strive to achieve these objectives. These specific applications will determine how democratic, unifying, or polarizing the system will be.

Why choose the objectives of society?

The most important thing about this system is the election of the objectives. Perhaps you are wondering right now: Why is it so important to choose the objectives of the society?

A society will be free, and it's members will be free only when all of its members can jointly and freely choose the reasons why they are together and willing to collaborate, when they choose the objectives that unite them, the circumstances they want to generate by being united and working together, the benefits they want to obtain from their union, the opportunities, possibilities, and freedoms that they want to generate, and what they are willing to give in return and the freedoms and powers they are willing to limit to achieve their objectives.

The persons or groups that decide the objectives of a society and how to achieve them, are deciding the reason why that society exists, the circumstances that society is and generates for its members, what people can and cannot do, for what goal the members of the society will work together and strive for, and the opportunities, possibilities, and benefits that society will generate for its members. If the objectives of society are decided by a powerful group, class, or person and imposed on all members of society, then the entire society works for these powerful people to achieve their objectives, and all the members of the society live and confront the circumstances generated by the common effort to achieve the objectives of the powerful. If people cannot choose the reason why they are in a society, the objective that unites them, for which they collaborate, work, and compete, then the society is not free, and the humans in that society are not free. If a person cannot choose the reason why he is in his society, the reason why he unites with other human beings, lives with them, collaborates, competes, and works with them, then that person does not have freedom.

In order for me to be free when I'm with you, I have to have my own reasons for being with you. I can only be free in a society I develop with you if I am able to decide on my own what I seek to obtain from our society. Our society can only be free If I recognize that it is necessary that you do the same, that you are free and can freely choose to be part of the society and what you want to get out of it. By uniting my objectives with your objectives, we can develop a society that works for the objectives of both; and we will both be free together and strive for our common goals.

If the citizen participates in the process of choosing the objectives of his society, and all the actions of the society are directed to achieve these objectives, then each action of the society will bring the citizen closer to his objectives. Working for these objectives, and the objectives themselves, generate the circumstances in which citizens will live. If citizens freely choose the objectives of society and work together to achieve them, then the circumstances and the world they generate with their efforts will be what they chose, what they strive for, and what their capacities managed to achieve. By choosing the objectives of his society, and by designing all the decisions and actions of the society to achieve these objectives, the citizen has in his own hands the circumstances in which he will live and develop.

Not all individuals in a society are experts in all subjects, not all of them will know how to achieve a result, or achieve an objective, or what the impacts of a law, action, or projects will be, but everyone knows, or has the ability to know, the world in which they would like to live, the circumstances in which they wish to live, in which they would like themselves, their children and the other members of society to develop and live. Everyone can know the opportunities, possibilities, and freedoms they would like to have. And if they don't know, allowing everyone the opportunity to think about and shape their own society based on their own objectives will empower them to think and decide about their objectives, their personal goals, and the objectives they want their society to have, the circumstances in which they would like to live, develop, and generate through the joint effort of all the members of society. Not everyone can achieve an objective, but everyone has the capacity to set an objective.

Everyone, from the most ignorant and illiterate person to the one with the most academic degrees, has the capacity to know or imagine what kind of world they would like to live in. Maybe they don't know how to get to it. Surely they don't know the world in which others would like to live, but they can know the world in which they, themselves, would like to live in. The Democratic Objectivecracy allows all members of society to set the objectives of their society; the world, the circumstances that their society aims to create, the world in which they want to live.

You don't have to know how to achieve an objective to know that you want to achieve it. It is not necessary to know how you are going to get an opportunity to know that you want to have that opportunity.

Let's develop a free society! Let's strive together to achieve the objectives of our partnership! What are you looking for in this society? What would you like society, that is, your effort together with that of all other citizens, to achieve? What are the reasons why you choose to be part of this society? What opportunities do you want your society to give you? What benefits? What freedoms? In what circumstances do you want to live? You can say:

- I want physical security, to know that my life and freedom, and those of the people I love, are secure; that all members of society are going to protect each other, that we will walk the streets and be safe, that we will not witness violence.

- I want health, that as much as possible, with the resources that we have, we seek to cure the sick with the medicines and treatments that we have available and that we will search and develop new cures, treatments, and medicines.

- I want economic opportunities, the opportunity to develop a business with other members of this society.

- I want time and resources for culture so that together with the other members of society we live, celebrate life, art, music, cuisine, and the traditions of our ancestors.

- I want infrastructure and public transport so that we can all travel, communicate, learn, work, do business, and collaborate with each other and with neighboring societies.

- I want everyone in my community to have enough food and nutrition.

- I want to protect the environment; that we share the planet polluting as little as possible, and developing in a sustainable way.

- I want to reverse the climate crisis.

- I want more economic equality; to create economic opportunities for everyone so that everyone can have economic growth, not just a few.

- I want...

The Democratic Objectivecracy gives the member of society the right to decide for what reason he will be part of the society; it gives each of its members the right to decide the objectives of their society.

You have the right to decide: I want to be in this society for this reason, to achieve this objective, to build and live in these circumstances, to have these opportunities and possibilities, and to have these freedoms and security.

On the other hand, the objective scale is not only used to guide and determine each action of the society and each law, but it is the metric by which the results of the laws and actions of the society are objectively evaluated and judged. If the result of an action or law does not get society closer to the objective for which the action was carried out, that action or law is suspended and a new one is developed. If a law has unforeseen consequences that go against one of the objectives, then that law is suspended and a new law is sought whose results align with the objectives.

There are many processes that a society can use to decide in a democratic way what its objectives are going to be, and many other ways that society can organize itself to work to achieve its objectives.

In the following pages, we will only propose one way to elect the objectives and one social organization system developed to achieve these objectives. Remember that you can agree with the basic principles of the Democratic Objectivecracy but not with the specific application we will propose. It is up to you to decide what you like, what you are convinced by, what you want to discard, modify, or change.

What do you think? Do you think that all people have the right to decide the objectives of their society? Do you think that all people have the right to decide the reason why they want to belong to a society? Do they have the right to decide what they want from their society, to decide under what circumstances they would like to live, and the circumstances the society strives to generate, even if they do not have the knowledge to achieve those objectives or to generate those circumstances? Do you think it is beneficial for society to have clear metrics to judge all public action, law, etc.? Why do you think that people should not choose the objectives of their society and the reason why they are part of a society?

Electing the objectives

What process could allow each and every individual in a society to participate with equal power, value, and weight to decide the objectives of their society?

There are many answers to this and I am sure you can think of other ways than the one I am going to propose. Analyze my proposal, think if you can improve it, or if you can develop a better method to choose the objectives of your society.

Democracy by Average

Democracy by Average is a democratic decision-making process in which the decisions of citizens are averaged to obtain the midpoint of society. This average is what all members of society have in common, or where their opposing views, ideas, and desires converge, and therefore becomes the decision of the society.

All social, political, and economic issues, or at least all the ones that are possible, are formulated and presented to society in such a way that the responses of citizens can be averaged. The questions are not presented in binary or multiple-choice form, but in such a way that an average can be obtained from individual answers.

In this system, there are no winners or losers, the majority does not win, the minority does not win, the winner does not rule over the loser. In this system, the responses of all citizens are averaged to obtain the average, the midpoint, the point of convergence, of what all the citizens want for their society.

Democratic Objectivecracy by Average

To democratically choose the objectives of society, I recommend averaging the objectives chosen by all its individual citizens. This means that each citizen, individually and freely, chooses the objectives he wants his society to have and all the objectives chosen by all individuals are averaged to determine the objectives of the whole society.

This means that I cannot impose my objectives on you, and you cannot impose your objectives on me. This also means that people do not vote directly to approve or disapprove a specific objective, and that the majority who wants a specific objective does not have the power to impose that objective on every other member of the society. Each person individually chooses the objectives they want their society to have and everyone's objectives are averaged to achieve the objectives of the society. This average is where the objectives of every single member of the society converge, where opposing ideas and objectives meet, it is the midpoint of what all citizens seek in common. This average is what unites society.

But how can we manage to average the objectives of every individual member of the society?

Example of a system that averages objectives:

There are many ways in which you can create a system to average the objectives of a society. Here is just one example, one option out of many that there might be.

In order to average the objectives of the whole society, the simplest thing is to give each person 100 points for their objectives and then each citizen makes a list of their objectives and assigns a percentage of the 100 points they has available. The more points an objective has, the more important it will be for society and the more resources will be dedicated to achieving that objective. The lists of each citizen are collected and the points assigned to each objective are averaged to obtain the average number of points that the whole society gives to each objective.

The society can also give people -100 points. That is, negative points to assign to negative objectives, what the citizen does not want in their society, what they want their society to combat or leave behind. If an objective is on both the positive and negative sides, then the difference between the two numbers is drawn and the result is what society is looking for.

For example:

1. Each citizen has 100 points to assign to their positive objectives and -100 to assign to negative objectives.

The positive objectives are the objectives that the individual wants their society to strive for, that will be the guide for their society. They are the circumstances that the individual wants their society to generate; the opportunities, possibilities, and freedoms that the person wants their society to generate; the benefits they wants to obtain by being part of society.

Negative objectives are things that the individual wants their society not to have, that she wants her society to fight against, or that she wants her society to leave behind. For example: Gender violence.

2. Each citizen assigns a percentage of these 100 points to the objectives they want. There can be as many objectives as the individual wants, however, the more objectives they choose, the lower percentage each one is assigned. The importance of an objective depends on the points assigned to it.

For example:

Free education: 30 points
Security: 30 points
Human rights: 10 points
Economic growth: 10 points
Economic equality: 10 points
Protection of the environment: 5 points
Social security: 5 points

Total: 100 points

3.   Citizens can also develop subcategories. By doing so, they can make their objectives more specific, at the same time uniting them with the broader objectives of the other citizens. A single objective can have two or more subcategories, and the points on each subcategory are added together to generate the total points for the entire category. This means that the citizen chooses specific objectives within the broader objectives.

For example: A citizen can set education as an objective, and free primary education and free high school education as sub-objectives. He can give free primary education twenty points and free high school ten points. These points go to the education category, so education has thirty points; but within the equation they will have their own category and will be averaged with the objectives of all the others who chose education as their objective and who established subcategories.

Example person 1:

Education:
Free primary education: 20
Free High School education: 10
Total to education: 30

Example person 2:

Education:
Free primary education: 10 points
Free High School education: 10 points
Higher education: 10 points
Continuing education: 10 points
Total to education: 40 points

The average is the society's objectives:

Total education: 35 points
Total free primary education: 15 points

Total free High School education: 10 points
Total higher education: 5 points
Total continuing education: 5 points

Each citizen can establish their own objective as specifically or as open as they likes. However, the more open an objective, the more likely it is that other citizens have chosen the same objective, and the more points that objective will have.

4. The objectives with their respective points are received by the electoral body, and an average is calculated among all the objectives of all the citizens to obtain a scale of objectives for the society. The average of all the objectives chosen by each individual establishes the objectives of the entire society. That is, the objectives of the society are the average of the objectives of the members of the society.

For example:

The economic growth category received 30% of all points in society. Among those who chose economic growth, most chose subcategories. Among those who chose subcategories for economic growth, the subcategory of economic equality obtained 20% of the total points of all society, and the free market obtained 10%. This means that society will aim for economic growth, and this economic growth must result in greater economic equality while allowing and promoting the free market. But the free market should not block economic equality, nor should the search for equality eliminate the free market completely. However, because economic equality has more points than free market, the society is going to invest more resources to generate economic equality and might take some actions to regulate the free market, without eliminating it.

5. There may be some objectives that some people establish as positive and others as negative. The average of these objectives will be the common objective for all of society.

6. In addition, it can also be decided that the objectives that have less than a certain percentage of the points of the entire society are not included in the objectives of the society. Each society must establish the minimum percentage that an objective must receive to be part of the society's objective.

For example, if an objective does not receive more than 0.1%, it does not become part of society's objectives.

In order to determine the minimum number of points needed to include an objective in the objective scale for the whole society, citizens can use the average democratic process. All citizens individually decide a minimum percentage that they deem necessary, and the answers of all of them are averaged to obtain the final number. That is the decision of the whole society.

For example:

When electing their objectives, citizens are also asked:
What is the minimum percentage an objective has to have in order to be included as an objective for the whole society? ____ %

Citizen 1 chose: 0.1%
Citizen 2 chose: 0.5%
Citizen 3 chose: 0.01%
Citizen 4 chose: 1%

Average, citizens decision: 0.4%

This means that objectives will have to have at least 0.4% of all the society's points to be able to be considered a social objective.

What are the benefits society gets from averaging individual's objectives?

1. When the objectives of every individual within society are averaged, it is very likely that the list of objectives of society will have at least something that every individual chose and that every individual thinks is important. Citizens will recognize some of their own objectives in the objectives of the society.

The objective scale of the whole society will be the average of all the objectives of all the members of the society so that each individual will be able to see and recognize in this list at least part of the objectives that he wants and chose for his society. Therefore he will be able to see what he has in common with all the other members of the society or where their interests coincide. Each individual will be able to identify the objectives they have chosen and will know that their objectives are the objectives of their society. So, with its efforts to achieve the societies objectives, the society as a whole always strives to achieve at least some of the objectives that each individual chose. The citizens will know that the whole of society is working to achieve the objectives he has in common with the other members of his society.

2. When an average of different categories is produced, there are no winners and losers, and no imbalances of power. Every single person, point, and objective has the same weight to influence the whole of society.

All the individuals have the same influence on the objectives of their society. There are no citizens who lose and are therefore completely excluded from the decision-making process. Every citizen influences the objectives of society in the same way. They all have the same 100 positive points and 100 negative points to assign to the objectives of their society.

Everyone participates, everyone decides, and there are no sides that lose completely or win completely. What guides society is the average, the midpoint, the convergence point of the objectives sought by every individual within the society.

While in a representative democracy or in a direct democracy by simple majority, there are losers that are not taken into account, when obtaining an average of the objectives of the society, all the members of the society are taken into account, without leaving anyone outside the decision-making process.

Each of the individuals decided what they are looking for in society and the union and average of all of them becomes the objectives of the society.

3.   Averaging what every citizen decided promotes social cohesion and avoids polarization:

In general, there are more things that people have in common and that can unite them than those that can divide them. A senior citizen, an evangelical Christian, a boomer, a millennial, and an atheist will all have different objectives, but some of these objectives will be similar for all of them, and society will work towards these common objectives. Everyone will be able to recognize the objectives they have in common and it is these objectives in common that everyone will work together to achieve.

By averaging the objectives of the society, the most polarized and extreme parts of the society will average each other out, and a midpoint will be obtained. The result of this will be that members of society will need to convince, and not condemn or demonize their opponents, because they do not require a simple majority to win, they have to convince as many people as possible to choose their objectives, knowing that anyone who is in opposition can use his negative points to subtract from, or eliminate, their objective. The way to ensure an objective becomes one of the society's objectives is by convincing and not by shunning, condemning, or dividing.

Social cohesion and a sense of unity will be generated when all members can recognize what they have in common with each other, where their interest intersect, and when they know that none of the factions, polarized groups, or powerful people, classes or groups have control over them; but they all have the same power, value, and the same weight when deciding the objectives of their society.

Whereas, in an electoral representative democracy, the elections generate losers that will not be taken into account during an elected official's administration, and therefore cause friction, opposition, and polarization, the system that averages the points given to each objective takes every single person into account and everyone has the same value and power to decide their society's objectives; as a result most members of society will not perceive themselves as governed by others, and they will perceive that their society is striving for common objectives.

Each member of society will be able to clearly see and know what the society as a whole is striving for, where it is going, the objectives for which all members of society unite, and those everyone strives to achieve.

The process in which every individual citizen has to decide every objective he wants for his society and chooses how many points to give to it, prevents the formation of homogeneous groups that develop group identity based on the differences they have with other groups; because each individual will know that she will have objectives in common with most of the other individuals she meets, but that her own list of objectives and the amount of points she assigns to each objective will most likely not be the same as that of any other individual. Each individual will know themselves to be unique inside society and will also identify where their objectives converge with those of all other members of their society. The process of choosing objectives for the society atomizes and focalizes the differences and the similarities that every person has with every other member of the society. The process of choosing how many points to assign to every objective personalizes the objective scale of each citizen to the point where it will not be exactly the same as that of any other citizen. Through the process of averaging every single person's objectives, every citizen will find where their individual objectives, interests, and desires meet those of every other citizen. This process will help citizens recognize themselves as individuals distinct from every other member of society but at the same time as part of a group of people with common objectives. Polarization is not avoided by eliminating the differences but by ensuring that everyone has differences, and that, even with those differences, all the members of the society can agree on common objectives for which to strive.

4. By asking people to choose objectives for their societies, their debates and elections will be based on specific ideas and objectives, and not on the character, abilities, capacity, history, or charisma of candidates.

In this new system, electoral debates and discussions will be centered around the objectives of society. They will be about ideas and not about candidates, their charisma, whether they have been corrupt or not, whether they are strong, weak, intelligent, or not. Discussions and debates about the direction of society will not be about the people who desire to be at the front of society, they will be about ideas and the objectives people want their societies to have.

The electoral representative democracy system generates campaigns in which the representatives, their character, their charisma, their historical record, and their capacity and credibility are as important, if not more important, than their ideas, their objectives, and their promises. Therefore, voters are often forced or tempted to choose only out of consideration for the candidates and not for their proposals and ideas. This problem will not exist when the citizens choose objectives, because there is no representative at the head of anything, people debate and choose objectives, ideas, ideals, not people. In an electoral representative democracy, elections and debates are a kind of popularity contest as much as about the future of the society. The new system will eliminate the popularity contest and every debate and election will be about ideas and objectives.

Naturally, there are some issues that cannot be averaged and that are very polarizing. In a later chapter we will expose a mechanism to identify and work on these issues in order to keep the polarization of society as low as possible.

Once we consider that all humans have the right to decide their reasons for participating in a free society and what they want to achieve by participating in this society. Do you think averaging the objectives of individuals is a democratic way of choosing the objectives of the entire society? Do you think that if everyone's objectives are averaged, we can obtain common objectives that unite us as a society?

Can you make your own list of objectives? Use your hundred positive points and one hundred negative points. What objectives would you like your society to have? What are the circumstances in which you would like to live? What benefits, opportunities, possibilities, and freedoms do you want your society to generate for all its citizens? Why?

Why choose objectives?

When a citizen chooses the objectives of his society, the citizen is deciding the reason why he is a member of society and the circumstances, opportunities, possibilities, freedoms, and benefits that he wishes to generate with the joint and common effort of his society.

When choosing the objectives of his society, the citizen says "This is what I want from my society. This is how I want my society to be. This is what I want my society to give me. This is what I want me and the other citizens to give to each other. This is the society I want to live in."

In addition, having clear objectives generates a clear metric to evaluate each decision and each action taken by society.

Why average the objectives of all the members of society?

By averaging the objectives of every individual, the society ensures that most citizens will recognize some of the objectives they chose in the common objectives of the society as a whole. This will give the citizen the certainty that his society is working for him and for his fellow citizens, and not against them and that society will not oppress him. There may be opposing opinions, however, most of those who have opposing opinions on one topic, have similar opinions to other citizens on other topics.

For example: A young woman may not have the same objective list as an old man. But usually, both of them will agree that their society needs security and education.

Furthermore, the average of the objectives balances the extremes of the members of a society. The objectives of the opposite ends of the population will cancel each other out and only the objectives they hold in common will remain. That is, the objectives that govern society will be the midpoint of the individual objectives of each member of society at any given time. The public life of the moment will be an average of the objectives of every individual at a set moment. These objectives will evolve to the extent and with the speed in which the points of view and positions of the members of society evolve.

Each objective gains more strength and budget if more people are convinced of the objective and loses strength if a sector of the population votes against it. In order to make an individual's objective part of society's objectives, those who seek the objective lose more by condemning the opposition and dividing the population, since they polarize and obtain negative points for the objective they seek. For an objective of a few people to become a social objective, they need to convince people, not divide and separate them. The path to change that each individual desires in a truly democratic and free society is to convince other citizens of the validity of an objective, not to fight against them. The path to change in a Democratic Objectivecracy by average is in discourse, debate, and convincing, not fear, force, oppression, and power.

The list of objectives of the society will not be identical to the list of objectives of any individual, but some of the objectives every citizen chose will be similar to the objectives of the rest of society, and therefore will be present in the ruling objective list. Each individual will be able to see part of himself and part of his interests and objectives in the objectives of the whole society. All citizens will be able to identify what they have in common, the goals they share with other citizens, in the goals of their society. The average of the objectives is the point where everyone's objectives meet and converge.

Why allow the objectives of society to be periodically changed in elections?

If circumstances change, the needs and objectives of a society might change. If members of the society learn and achieve certain objectives, they may want new objectives in the future or they might realize that certain objectives no longer interest them. On the other hand, the concept of morality and justice evolve over time and it is natural that with this evolution certain objectives of society will evolve.

If only one generation of people can set the objectives of society and do not allow new generations to choose their own objectives for their society, then the society will be oppressive to the new generations. All members of society must be able to establish the objectives for their society, the reason why they want to belong to the society and the type of society it will be. In fact, even if a person chooses the objectives, but with the passage of time he acquires knowledge and experiences that lead him to change his mind about what the objectives of society should be, and the social structure does not give him the opportunity to choose and change these objectives, then the system becomes an oppressive structure. Society must allow periodic selection of objectives to allow the course of society to evolve and change, just as the members of society change their minds and evolve their thoughts and ideas.

CHAPTER 5

Social Structure

Once you have the list of objectives ordered by their importance to the society, you have to decide what to do to achieve the objectives. How will these objectives be achieved? How will society organize itself to work towards these objectives? There are many ways in which the members of a society can unite and organize themselves to work for their common objectives, some of them more traditional and hierarchical, and others more innovative and democratic.

So far, we have combined two types of democracy: The Democratic Objectivecracy and Average Democracy. These two processes are designed to take decisions and determine the objectives of a society, but not to achieve these objectives. To make laws and execute the necessary actions and projects to achieve the objectives of the society, it is necessary to generate a structure that allows action.

This structure can be more or less democratic and more or less effective. For example, once the objectives of the society are decided through average democracy, the society can organize itself to achieve its objectives through an epistocracy or a technocracy. This would be a system in which all citizens participate in the process of choosing the objectives of their society and the experts in each subject have to achieve these objectives. However, this would not be a completely democratic social structure, it would not be participatory, and power would concentrate in the hands of the technocrats. Therefore, I do not recommend it.

I recommend combining even more types of democracy to develop a truly democratic and efficient social organization system. Remember a democratic system is one that organizes the citizens so that they can govern themselves. For example, we can combine democracy by lottery with direct and participatory democracy to obtain a completely new type of society. This new society will be truly democratic and have all the characteristics that we have previously established that we want our new system to have. Our current social structure did not exist before, therefore it is natural that today we develop a new form of social structure with which we can organize tomorrow.

I am sure that you are going to be able to think and develop different applications and ways in which we can organize a Democratic Objectivecracy. The social organization system I propose, or any other social organization system, can improve if more and more people are thinking, questioning, debating, and implementing the system. Analyze my proposal and if you find a way to improve it, have doubts, criticisms, or think of a better way of organizing a Democratic Objectivecracy, please share them with me and with the people around you.

Remember that you can agree with the basic principle of Democratic Objectivecracy and Average Democracy and not agree with the following social structure that I will propose. The following social structure is just one of many ways in which the Democratic Objectivecracy can be applied in the world in which we live.

The government structure we currently have is representative and this means that representatives act and decide on behalf of other citizens. This structure is vertical and this means that it operates within a hierarchy in which the people who occupy the highest positions in the hierarchy have the power to give orders, command, and govern, and the people below obey. One of the reasons we want to change the social system is to get rid of such hierarchies where authorities and rulers, who in fact do not represent their constituencies, hold too much power. For this reason, from now on we will eliminate the entire structure of the electoral representative democracy. From this moment on, stop thinking about presidents, prime ministers, governors, mayors and legislators because they will not exist in our new society.

New Social Structure

Once the objectives of the society have been chosen through the average democratic process, society has to act in order to achieve its objectives. We have established that in our new social structure power will not be concentrated in a few hands, in our new social structure the majorities will not have the power to oppress the minorities nor will the minorities have the power to oppress the majorities. We want all citizens to have power, we want them to have the responsibility and to be encouraged and incentivized to participate and strive to achieve the societies' objectives and we want the new social structure to be very hard or impossible to corrupt. With all these requirements in mind, the structure of the new society will be a combination of democracy by lottery, direct democracy, and participatory democracy.

This proposal of how to organize society is completely new. The most important part of this structure is that the objectives of the society are democratically chosen by all its citizens. Once the objectives have been determined, the citizens can propose laws, actions, and projects designed to achieve the society's objectives. Citizens' proposals are evaluated by an Assembly of citizens selected by lottery. This is the Administrative Assembly and its main job is to collect taxes and manage the resources of the society. This Assembly makes public tenders to receive proposals from the citizens for laws, projects, or actions designed to achieve the objectives of the society. The members of the assembly evaluate the projects according to their effectiveness and the objectives of the society and then decide which project to approve and give financing to. The Administrative Assembly's decision-making process and the results of the citizens' projects that were approved and financed are monitored, evaluated, and judged by another citizens' assembly. This is the Assembly of Auditors, and its job is to make sure that the decisions of the Administrators do not go against the objectives of the society, that they are not corrupt and that they are competent. They will also monitor, evaluate, and judge the performance, results, and adherence to the objectives of the projects and the laws put into action by the approved citizen tenderers.

In this society, it is the citizens who propose the laws, projects, and actions to achieve the objectives that all the members of society have in common; it is an Assembly of Administrators made up of citizens chosen by lottery, which reviews, deliberates, evaluates, approves, and decides to finance the proposals of the citizens; and it is the Assembly of Auditors, made up of citizens chosen by lottery, which evaluates the decision-making process of the Administrators and the results of the laws, projects, and actions approved, financed, and put into operation to achieve the objectives of the society.

This new society combines different types of democracy:

- The Democratic Objectivecracy by Average to choose the objectives of the society.

- Democracy by lottery to assign citizen Assemblies to deliberate and make decisions based on the objectives chosen by all citizens.

- Direct and Participatory Democracy to involve citizens in all actions of society through tenders. All actions to achieve the objectives of the society are proposed by citizens through tenders and the Administrators decide which proposal of the citizens is the most effective to achieve the objectives of the society and the Auditors judge the results of these actions.

- Direct and Participatory Democracy to modify proposals of the Assemblies or to modify proposals of other citizens that the members of the Assemblies approved.

- Direct Democracy to veto a decision of the Assemblies. If enough citizens are against a decision of the Assemblies, their decision is blocked. Citizens can always have the last word. They do not need to approve and vote for everything, but if they so desire, they can join together to veto an Assembly decision.

- The democratic principle of horizontal organization. There is no government, only Administrators who approve the proposals of the citizens and Auditors who judge its results. All actions are carried out by the citizens themselves and can be vetoed by the citizens themselves.

Each administration is made up of five parts:

1. The objectives

2. The Assembly of Administrators

3. The Citizen tenderers

4. The Assembly of Auditors

5. All electing citizens

CHAPTER 6

The Scale of Objectives

The core and center of the new social structure are the objectives of society freely chosen by its citizens. The entire social structure is designed to enable the citizens to freely and democratically choose their society's objectives; to set up mechanisms and structures to determine in a democratic and efficient way the actions, projects, and laws designed to achieve the society's objectives; and to ensure that the social structure is just, difficult to corrupt, efficient, stable, does not allow abuses of power, provides equal opportunities for all citizens, and unifies the members of society in pursuit of their common objectives.

There are different processes through which the scale of objectives of the society can be obtained. The most effective and democratic process is that of Democracy by Average. This process averages the objectives chosen individually by each member of the society to determine the common objectives of all the members of the society. These objectives are the circumstances in which citizens want to live and that they want to generate for themselves and for all members of society through collaboration and joint effort. The circumstances that society generates for all its members covers topics such as physical security, food security, health, the economy, labor rights, education, the opportunities available to all members of society, freedoms, rights, and the duties of all, the services and infrastructure that society provides for its citizens, the regulation or prohibition of certain actions or behaviors, the environmental or social impact of production, commerce, and consumption activities, the limitations of power, etc. In choosing the objectives of society, citizens choose the objectives for which the joint efforts of all members of society will be invested.

For example, some members of society may choose free education, security, economic growth and equality, and preservation of culture and traditions as the objectives for their society to have.

Objectives can be both positive and negative. Positive objectives are the circumstances that members of society have and want to conserve, or do not have and want to obtain; and the negative objectives are the circumstances that citizens have and want to leave behind or that they do not have but consider it necessary for society to take actions to avoid and prevent generating those specific circumstances.

We will now propose a social structure that will allow societies to be organized in a democratic and efficient way. It will be a social structure in which the citizens themselves propose the projects, actions, and laws that will lead society to achieve its objectives; one in which one assembly of citizens, elected by lottery, choose among the proposals presented by citizens and another assembly of citizens, elected by lottery, review the selection process and evaluate and judge the results of the projects and the laws. In this system, there is no government and power is not concentrated in a few hands, but there is social organization and collaboration that allows society to achieve its objectives and to expand the possibilities, opportunities, and freedoms of all members of society.

CHAPTER 7

Administrators Assemblies and Committees

The first body of the organization of the society is the Administrator's Assembly. This Assembly is in charge of managing society's resources according to the scale of objectives. Within the Assembly, committees are formed that are assigned to specific topics. These committees are in charge of analyzing and choosing between the tenders that citizens proposed to carry out actions to achieve the objectives of society. This Assembly of Administrators does not present or develop its own proposals, it only evaluates the proposals of the citizens and its job is to choose the proposals that will be most effective in achieving the objectives of society. All their decisions are reviewed by the Assembly of Auditors and can be questioned and vetoed by citizens.

The functions of the Administrators are:

1. Administrators collect taxes or contributions from individuals and companies for society.

There are many ways in which society can be financed. It is up to each society to identify its monetary system, how it is going to finance its projects, what type of taxes it is going to demand and from which sectors of society, etc. The method of choosing taxes can also be democratic. In fact, if taxes are not decided democratically, the society is not free, because citizens are being forced to dedicate part of their time and effort to generating wealth that they have to give to the government. But if citizens democratically choose the objectives of their society and democratically choose the amount of time and wealth they are willing to contribute to achieve these objectives, then taxes are a collective decision of the citizens themselves and not an imposition on them. A very democratic way to decide how many taxes each person will have to pay is by using the principles of Democracy by Average.

For example: A system can be developed to determine the taxes by averaging what every citizen thinks the taxes should be for every sector of the population or every type of product. That is, a system in which each member of society presents what he thinks is a fair tax on every economic sector of the society and every individual proposal is averaged to obtain the percentage of taxes that society will ask from its citizens.

The society is divided into economic levels according to their wealth. Each individual in the society proposes a percentage that they think should be applied as taxes to each economic level. The individual proposals are then averaged to determine the tax for each sector of the population.

For example: Society is divided into ten economic levels. Where one is the poorest and ten the richest. Each citizen proposes a tax for each level, and the average of what every member of society proposed will determine the taxes for each level of the population. If all the people decide that 0% of taxes should be applied to their poorest levels of the population, then the poorest in society will not pay taxes. If, for the fifth economic level one person proposes 15% and another 35%, then the average, that is, the tax for the 5th level will be 25%. Taxes for each economic level of the population will be the average of what each individual in society decides.

Income Level of the population	Proposal: Person 1	Proposal: Person 2	Proposal: Person 3	Proposal Person 4	Proposal Person 5	Average taxes

1 Poorest	0%	0%	0%	0%	0%	0%
2	5%	0%	10%	3%	2%	4%
3	8%	5%	15%	5%	5%	8.6%
4	10%	8%	20%	10%	10%	11.6%
5	15%	10%	25%	15%	15%	16%
6	20%	15%	30%	25%	20%	23%
7	30%	15%	35%	30%	25%	27%
8	40%	15%	40%	35%	35%	33%
9	50%	15%	45%	40%	40%	38%
10 richest	60%	15%	55%	50%	50%	46%

Of course, regulation could be put in place that will not allow the tax to generate so great a burden that the members of one level are pulled down to a lower level. The tax on level 6 cannot be so big as to make people on level 6 have the same amount of wealth as those on level 5.

To help citizens dimensionalize the wealth each sector of the economy has, and how that wealth will be affected by the taxes they propose, the amount of wealth each sector of the population and the amount of people in each sector of the population should be included and given to the citizens. They should also be able to see how their proposed taxes affect the wealth of each sector of the population.

For example:

Level 10, the richest among society: yearly earnings or gains of 1,000,000,000 or more.
Percentage of the population in this sector: 1%
Tax decided by the citizens: 46%
Total wealth of level 10 of the population after taxes: 540,000,000 or more.

Another way to decide the amount of taxes is to divide the products and not the population into sectors, from basic and necessary products to exclusive and luxurious products. Each member of the society assigns a tax percentage to each product sector. Each individual's choice of tax is averaged to determine the tax on each sector of products.

This proposal is described at length in the book: The Democratic Economy of an Objectivecracy.

There are many ways in which funding can be raised for organization, administration, and public actions. Each society must develop its own way of democratically deciding how this financing will be raised.

2. Administrators invest the society's resources according to the scale of objectives.

Each objective on the objective scale has a percentage of the points it received from all its citizens. Each objective receives the percentage of funds from the public treasury equal to the percentage of points it received.

For example: If education was assigned 40% of all society's points and security 20%, the Administrators will assign 40% of public resources to education and 20% to security.

The number of points the citizens assign to each objective will be the amount of resources available to achieve the objective.

3. Administrators tender public funds according to the scale of objectives.

Administrators will not legislate and will not take concrete actions. Administrators will open tenders and it will be up to citizens to compete with each other to obtain funds from the public treasury to carry out actions and projects or design "collective contracts" to achieve the objectives of society. Administrators evaluate the projects they receive through tenders and decide which to approve and finance.

If education is assigned 40% of public funds, individual citizens, schools, universities, and law firms may participate in the tender to obtain part of these funds. Administrators are responsible for evaluating the projects presented and choosing among them.

The evaluation criteria are:

1. Their adherence to the objectives chosen by citizens.
2. Its efficiency: resources = results.
3. Its viability.
4. The history of projects previously implemented by the tenderers.

The selection process and the reasons for choosing one and not another project are completely transparent and public. Throughout the process, all tendering projects are open to the public so that they can evaluate and judge the Administrators' decisions. Administrators have to justify their decisions by answering the following questions:

1) How does the proposal chosen by the Administrative Assembly adhere to and promote the scale of objectives more than the other proposals of the other tenderers?

2) What is the direct cost of said proposal?
    i) How much money or resources have to be allocated from the public purse?

3) What is the indirect cost of said collective agreement or project?

    i)   What are the indirect costs of such public contracts, for example the environmental impact, the loss of opportunities, the increase in inequality, the impact on the health of members of society, the impact on the economy, etc.?

4) What are the projected results of the public contract or project?

    i)   The benefits will be established according to different projections of results taking into account different circumstances.

        (1) First projection: according to such circumstances the results are expected to be...

        (2) Second projection: according to these other circumstances, the results are expected to be ...

        (3) Third projection: according to other circumstances, the results are expected to be unsatisfactory and therefore the project is no longer viable and should be canceled.

5) What are the possible negative and positive side effects of the collective contract and how likely are they?

        (1) Negative or positive effects are measured according to the objective scale.

        (2) What actions will be taken to avoid or control these possible negative results?

        (3) What actions will be taken to correct the contract or project if these negative results appear?

        (4) At what point or with what negative results is the project considered to be no longer viable and is stopped?

6) Has the project been implemented with previous administrations and objective scales? If yes, with what results?

        (1) There are projects that can work with various administrations, as their objective may be present during many administrations. For these projects, the results they had in previous administrations will also be taken into consideration.

> (a) A school may seek funding through various administrations and use the results obtained during one administration as an argument in favor of requesting funds from the next administration.

7) Which individuals or groups propose and/or carry out the public contract or the project?

> (1) Has this individual or group done projects before? If yes, what were the results?

8) A detailed budget of absolutely all expenses of the project or collective contract.

> (1) Including items where costs can vary according to circumstances.

Once a collective contract or project is approved by the Administrators, they present it to the part of the population that will be most affected by the collective contract or project and subsequently a period of time is designated in which citizens can get involved to modify a project or collective contract on par with the citizens that won the tender. After this period of modification, the Administrators reassess the project, its efficiency, its viability, its adherence to the objective scale, the projected results and, according to their analysis, they can approve it or not. If the Administrators approve the project, they publish and distribute it to all citizens, and during a specific period of time all citizens can evaluate and judge the proposal. During this period, citizens can gather signatures to veto a project or collective contract. If the citizens do not veto the project or collective agreement, then the administrators sign or finance it on behalf of all the citizens. These projects are now the actions and institutions that were previously the actions and institutions of the government. Citizens are the ones who take all the actions, not the administrative structure. Citizens are the ones who strive and work for their objectives. Citizens are involved in each process and can participate as they much as they want with their projects.

Every citizen can participate in their society wherever and as much as they want to since they can tender to develop collective contracts and projects, and if their projects are not approved they can participate by modifying the approved projects or vetoing them.

1.   Administrators sign public or collective contracts on behalf of all citizens.

What we now call "Laws" will disappear and collective contracts will take their place. These collective contracts are drawn up by citizens and companies to achieve a social objective. Then they participate in a public tender where the administrators evaluate each proposed collective contract including the cost and possible results, and decide which one will be approved, funded, and signed in the name of all the members of the society.

Each collective contract must establish the objective for which it works and the projection of results for said contract. If, after being approved and signed, a collective contract does not meet its projections, or has side effects that negatively affect one of the objectives within the objective scale, said contract will be revoked by the Assembly of Auditors.

Administrators evaluate all collective contract proposals and have a budget to hire experts on the issues of each contract to help them evaluate the proposals. They can also do their own field research and consult and deliberate with the sectors of the population that will be most affected by the collective contract.

Once the administrators have chosen a collective contract, they have to identify the sectors of the population that will be most affected by said collective contract and open with them a process in which the collective contract can be modified. The company that won the tender and elaborated the proposal for the original collective contract, works together with the sectors of the population that will be most affected by these contracts, and together they modify the proposal of the collective contract. Administrators have to evaluate the resulting contract according to the scale of objectives and decide whether to approve it or not. Once approved by the Administrators, the collective contract is published and all citizens will have a period of time during which they can evaluate it and, if a considerable percentage of citizens do not agree with the collective contract, they can veto it or request that a section of the contract be modified. If citizens do not veto the collective contract, Administrators sign it on behalf of all citizens.

It is very important to give citizens veto power over collective contracts, but not ask them to vote to approve collective contracts. Because if all citizens have to vote all the time, then we will have the same problem as with direct democracy and all citizens will be overwhelmed by the number of collective contracts that they have to review. However, if they don't have to approve and vote on every contract, but retain the power of veto, citizens don't have to get involved if they don't want to, but the power remains in their hands.

The approved collective contract will now be part of the terms and conditions of the social contract and the circumstances in which all citizens will develop. This collective agreement will determine what is allowed, what is prohibited, what is stimulated, incentivized, and what is discouraged within society.

These collective contracts will not be like the current laws imposed on citizens, chosen by the ancestors or by the representatives of one sector of the population. These collective contracts will be designed to achieve the objectives of society and will be developed by groups of citizens, modified by the citizens who are more affected by it, and approved by all citizens.

Once the collective contract is signed, the auditors will begin to assess the impact of the contract, whether the results are as projected in the tender or not, and whether they have unwanted side effects.

It is very important to change the name laws to collective contract, because the word law has an absolute connotation. On the contrary, collective contract communicates that it is something developed by humans and that might change.

CHAPTER 8

Tenderers

They are the citizens or private entities that apply to obtain public funds to carry out an action, project, or develop a collective contract. Any citizen or private entity that is not part of the administration in turn or the previous one and that has not been found guilty of acts of corruption, defrauding society, or certain crimes, can participate as a tenderer.

The tenderers' projects cover all the areas in which society is involved and which previously belonged to the state, except for the courts where the Auditors will judge the Administrators, the tenderers, and the citizens for breaking collective and private contracts. All other areas in which governments are usually involved will be in the charge of the tenderers. This means that everything from the writing of collective contracts (formerly laws), to security and education, will be in the hands of citizens or groups that propose their projects to Administrators and are kept in check by the Auditors.

Citizens through Democracy by Average decide the objectives of their society and the financing they are going to assign to each objective, and then the citizens themselves propose projects, actions, or collective contracts to achieve these objectives.

It is the responsibility of each society to establish what type of companies or groups are entitled to tender. To protect society from economic inequality that generates power inequality inside a society, measures are recommended, such as asking that all companies that apply for tenders be collectives; that the projects do not generate dividends; and that the salaries of the members maintain a certain proportion between the least paid and the best paid persons.

For example, the highest paid people in each project cannot earn more than 10 times an hour what the least paid person in the company earns.

It is up to each society to decide who will be able to participate in the public tenders and under what circumstances, whether they will be collectives or capitalist enterprises, whether or not they can generate dividends with the projects financed by the society, etc.

The tenderers have to justify their project, explaining:

1) For which objective or objectives of the objective scale they will work.

2) The actions, the people involved, and the work to be done.

3) How they will carry out said work and actions.

4) How these actions will not negatively affect the other objectives of the society.

5) Possible negative side effects, according to the scale of objectives, that if they were to appear, the project would have to be suspended.

6) What are the project's concrete and measurable projected results in the short, medium, and long term. The project will be evaluated by the administrators based on said projections; and the results of the project will be judged by the Auditors based on these projections.

7) What is the cost of the project and the detailed budget where public funds are to be used?

To be chosen, the projects will be evaluated by the administrators according to the relation between cost and benefit. This means that the projects will be evaluated according to the cost of the project and the projected results. If, in order to win, a tender presents projections that are too optimistic or unrealistic, and the project does not achieve its projections, the project might be approved by the Administrators but it will later be   judged by the Auditors and may be revoked; furthermore, depending on the circumstances and the difference between the projections and the results, the bidder could be subjected to a trial for defrauding the society.

For example: If a tenderer only reaches 70% of its projected results, the project or collective contract is revoked. But if the project only reaches 50% or less of its projected results, the contract is revoked and the circumstances of the failure of said project investigated, with the possibility that the tenderer will be sued for defrauding the citizens.

8) Conflicts of interest, nepotism, and extra benefits. Each project has to explicitly identify if the tenderers or their relatives have something extra to gain, directly or indirectly, in addition to the project or collective contract. If these benefits or relationships are not presented in the tenders and then it is found that the tenderer, his relatives, or acquaintances are being disproportionately benefited over the rest of the population by the project, the tenderer may be accused of corruption or defrauding society.

   a) The tenderer has to state, when he presents the project, if he is going to work with family or friends and the reason for doing so.

   b) The tenderer has to stipulate whether family or friends will be subcontracted or benefited more than other citizens.

   c) The fact that family or friends are benefited by a contract or project is not necessarily a bad thing, in fact it can be a very good thing because family and acquaintances can be the reason that motivates the individual to work for the project.

For example: a person can open a center for people with disabilities because their child or a relative has a disability.

There are two main types of tenders, collective contracts, and the implementation of specific actions and projects to achieve the objectives of the society.

1)   Collective Contracts

Collective contracts replace what we currently call laws. By changing the method by which they are developed, that is, the citizens themselves develop and modify them to meet their common objectives, and by changing the method by which they are applied or enforced, the concept of Law ceases to make sense and it is replaced by the concept of "Collective agreement" or "Collective Contract". This is a contract that all members of a society sign. It is not something imposed on them, but something freely chosen and developed by citizens. By choosing the objectives of society, citizens choose the objectives of their collective contracts and, through tenders, citizens themselves develop the terms and conditions they establish to achieve this objective. The collective contract is a contract that each citizen member of a society enters into with absolutely every other citizen member of the society.

Private entities or citizens can present projects that include investigation of the current situation and preparation or modification of collective contracts to encourage or limit certain behaviors of society according to the objectives of the society.

There are some collective contracts that affect the entire population and others that only affect citizens who wish to have the right to carry out certain actions. The ideal would be to reduce as much as possible the collective contracts that apply to the entire society and make more specific contracts which give certain rights or permits to citizens who want to do a certain action, but in exchange commit to certain terms and conditions with the rest of the society.

For example: Instead of a traffic law, a collective contract is developed that must be signed by those who want to have the right to use a car. In order for a person to obtain his driving license, he must personally sign a contract that he enters into with the rest of society, A contract in which he commits to certain obligations and rules in order to obtain the right to drive a car through the streets that society shares and finances. This is a contract that an individual enters into with the rest of society in order for the rest of society to give him the permission, privilege, or right to perform a certain action that can affect them all and that is possible thanks to their joint effort.

2)   Implementation of specific actions and projects

Instead of government programs, institutions, actions and executive power, citizens participate in tenders to propose specific actions and projects to achieve the common objectives of the entire society. Private entities or citizens can present projects that include investigation of the current situation and implementation of specific actions according to the objectives of societies.

For example:
1. Construction and maintenance of infrastructure: streets, bridges, highways, etc.
2. Social security system
3. Security guards
4. Criminal investigative agencies
5. Educational institutions, etc.

This does not mean that the resources or services are private, but it does mean that those responsible for administering, distributing, using, generating, or providing the resources or services will be citizens.

For example, a company will not own the streets of a city, but it does participate in a tender to build, pave, or maintain the streets of the city in good condition.

A company will not own the society's water, but a company may be in charge of building the drainage system, and they or another company may be in charge of maintaining the system.

All the actions and results of these companies will be evaluated and judged by the Auditors Assembly and by the citizens who, if they wish, can organize to veto or revoke a tender.

Tenders allow citizens to be involved in absolutely all of society's processes and projects. Citizens are the ones who work for society to achieve the objectives that they themselves choose. Every citizen has the opportunity and the incentives to compete to get involved in the area of their choice. The structure or administration of society retains little power over the citizens. With this type of organization, you can generate a lot of social action, a lot of collaboration among all members of society, a lot of work to achieve the objectives of society and large scale projects with great impact, while keeping the power of the social structure limited. Power is distributed in such a way that no one can use it to oppress. With this system, there is no government that imposes in a hierarchical way that governs from top to bottom, in which all the power of society is concentrated in a few hands. In the new system, power is distributed horizontally. With this system, there is no government. Instead, there is a social organization with the ability to collaborate and carry out small and large social actions and projects. This new system eliminates government and increases social organization and collaboration.

CHAPTER 8

Auditors

In addition to the Administrator's Assembly, the new social structure will have the Auditor's Assembly whose function is to collect information, analyze, evaluate, and judge all the actions of the administrators and tenderers according to the objectives of the society. All actions of administrators and tenderers will be monitored, evaluated, and judged by the auditors; who have the right to revoke tenders, projects, or collective contracts according to the following criteria:

1) Use of public funds for functions, actions, projects, or contracts not established in the original tender.

2) Corruption and/or lack of transparency.
   i) Use of influence and discretion not contemplated in the tender.
   ii) Disproportionate earnings for the tenderer, a relative, or friend not presented in the tender.

3) Efficacy:
   i) The results of tenders, projects, and collective contracts are evaluated at least once a year.
   ii) If tenders do not meet their projections by at least 70%, they are revoked. (70% is an arbitrary number, each society must decide what is the minimum efficiency it will allow in its projects. This can be decided using Average Democracy, when deciding their objectives, citizens are asked to determine the

minimum percentage of efficiency necessary for a tender to keep on working and the amount of inefficiency permitted before a fraud investigation is prompted. The answer of every citizen will be averaged to obtain the collective decision.)

iii)   If the tenders do not meet their projections by at least 50%, the Auditors can investigate the causes of said discrepancy between projections and results; and if they see it as appropriate, they can sue and put the tenderers on trial for corruption or defrauding the society. If the set of projects and collective contracts of an administration does not comply with at least 70% efficiency, the administration is investigated with the possibility of removing it from office.

iv)   If an Administrator or a tenderer is found to be corrupt, they are sued.

4) Secondary or unforeseen effects of the implementation of a project contrary to the objectives of the administration.

i)   The Auditors will have to evaluate the projects according to their results, even unforeseen side effects, and according to them decide to revoke or not a collective contract or project. In some cases, a collective contract or a project might meet all its objectives but generate other side effects that go against other objectives of the society. In this case, the Auditors must stop or revoke the tender.

Audit of the Auditors

To ensure that the Auditors carry out their work properly and do not fall into the temptation of corruption or inaction, it is recommended that at the end of each period of each administration, a third assembly be created that will be responsible for officially evaluating the results of both assemblies whose turn has ended. This third assembly will be formed through random selection among the members of previous assemblies, except those of the period immediately preceding. That is, the current Administrators are monitored and judged by the Auditors and the Auditors on duty are judged by the past Auditors and by all the citizens.

Citizen Complaint

Citizens may file a complaint about the decisions or actions of the Administrators or bidders before the Auditor Assembly. The Auditors designate a committee to investigate the complaint, and the committee presents its resolution to the Assembly, which decides whether or not to pursue the citizen's complaint. If the citizens are not satisfied with the judgment of the Auditors, they must gather a certain number of dissatisfied citizens and, once this number is gathered, they can appeal to an assembly made up of Auditors from previous assemblies. This group of citizens presents their complaint to this assembly made up of Auditors from previous administrations who evaluate the complaint and decide whether to act or not. If citizens are not satisfied with the decision of previous assemblies, they may request a vote of no confidence on the Auditors and Administrators.

If this vote of no confidence is voted by a considerable number of the citizens (example: 40%) then the members of the present assemblies will be removed from their positions and new selections will be carried out by lottery. However, the objective scale remains intact. The minimum approval required for an assembly to keep functioning is determined by the members of the society through the Average Democratic process. Each election cycle, every citizen proposes a percentage of disapproval required to disband an assembly and the proposals of all citizens are averaged.

The Assembly of Auditors has the faculty and the budget to appoint and contract investigators with specific knowledge and expertise to help them gather information for specific objectives.

Trials

One of the main tasks of auditors is to be in charge of the entire trial system of the society. Before a trial begins, judges are selected by lot from the Assembly of Auditors and juries are composed of citizens chosen by lot. Collective contracts must already have the penalties and sanctions for each type of breach or default. Therefore, the accusers have to prove that the accused did not comply with a clause of his contract and, if found guilty, they are assigned the sanction established in the contract itself.

There are 5 types of trials:

1) Trials of a tenderer for breach or default of a collective agreement, corruption, or defrauding the society.

2) Trials of a member of the Administrative Assembly for breach or default of a collective contract, corruption, or defrauding the society.

3) Trials of a member of the Assembly of Auditors for breach or default of a collective contract, corruption, or fraud.

4) Trials of a citizen for breach or default of a collective contract.

5) Trials of a citizen, tenderer, private entities, or members of assemblies for breach or defaults of private contracts.

Each of these trials is handled in a different way:

1) Trials of a tenderer for breach or default of a collective agreement, corruption, or defrauding the society.

The Auditors are in charge of monitoring the approved projects and the results of said projects. Within the Assembly of Auditors, committees are appointed to monitor and review a certain number of specific projects. When committee members discover that a tenderer is committing an act of corruption, is in breach of its contract, or is defrauding society, they file a legal case against him based on the collective contracts and individual contracts signed by the tenderers. Once the case against the tenderer has been built, the trial against him starts. These trials are preceded by a small committee of judges selected by lottery from among the Auditors who do not belong to the committee accusing the bidder. The juries are made up of citizens chosen by lottery.

Lawsuits can be filed by Auditors, citizens, or private entities with their respective teams of lawyers. Defenders may be represented by defense teams, whether they are lawyers or not.

Basically, when the members of a committee of Auditors detect fraud or a breach of the tenderers' contract, they set up a case with a team of lawyers or investigators and present it in a trial. The trial is presided over by judges selected by lottery among the members of the Assembly of Auditors; a jury of citizens selected by lottery is in charge of giving the final verdict and accused tenderers can hire a defense team to defend themselves against the allegations.

2)   Trials of a member of the Administrative Assembly for breach or default of a collective contract, corruption, or defrauding the society.

The Auditors are monitoring and evaluating the decisions and actions of the Administrative Assembly; if they discover that one or a group of Administrators is committing acts of corruption, fraud, or breaking collective contracts, they have to build a case against them and bring them to trial.

These trials are preceded by a small committee of judges randomly selected from among the Auditors. The trial against administrators will have a jury made up of citizens chosen by lottery.

3)   Trials of a member of the Assembly of Auditors for breach or default of a collective contract, corruption, or fraud.

The work of the Auditors is also evaluated by citizens in general, and if enough citizens come together to accuse an Auditor, a new committee of Auditors is formed which is made up of citizens who belonged to previous Assemblies of Auditors and Administrators. This committee must evaluate the accusations against the Auditor and decide if they proceed or not. To proceed, they set up a case against the Auditor. These trials are preceded by a small committee of judges randomly selected from among Auditors of past periods, excluding the period immediately preceding. The trial against Auditors will have a jury made up of citizens chosen by lottery.

4)   Trials of a citizen who is not a member of assemblies or is not a tenderer, for breach or default of a collective contract.

The police, or whoever takes over the police functions, or even a citizen can accuse another of a breach of a collective contract and bring him to trial. These trials are preceded by a small committee of judges randomly selected from among the Auditors and will have a jury of citizens chosen by lot. In these trials a citizen, a group of citizens, or the organization that supplants the police, files a lawsuit against a citizen who did not fulfill the collective contract. The accused citizen may have a defense team.

In later chapters, we will propose a new way to envision public security without police.

5)   Trials of a citizen, tenderer, private entities, or members of assemblies for breach or breach of private contracts.

In addition to collective contracts, citizens also enter into private contracts with each other. Citizens can also accuse another citizen of breaching a private contract and bring them to trial. In these cases, the judgments are presided over by a small committee of judges randomly selected from the Auditors and the jury will be made up of citizens selected by lot.

Trials and verdicts are open to public scrutiny. If a majority of citizens collect signatures to overturn the verdict of the jury and judges, the trial is overturned. If the majority of citizens do not unite against the verdict, the judge and the jury, in turn, on behalf of all citizens, sign the judgment. Again, in these cases citizens do not have to participate and can trust the system and the other citizens selected by lot, but if they wish, or notice inconsistencies, all citizens have the power to stop and veto actions and verdicts of the courts. If a verdict is vetoed, the trial is repeated with a new jury and chaired by a new body of judges.

CHAPTER 9

Citizens

A free society is made up of individuals who freely choose whether or not they want to belong to a society, who decide what kind of society they aspire to have, what benefits and assurances they want to obtain from their society, and what they are willing to renounce, to sacrifice, give or do, to be able to belong to the society and for their society to be what they want it to be. A free society is a joint project that members of society freely undertake. The Democratic Objectivecracy is a system through which a free society can be organized, where citizens decide whether or not they are part of society, the objectives of their society, and what they will do together or individually to achieve these objectives.

In this new way of organizing a society, citizens receive all possible economic and social incentives to participate in their society's efforts to achieve their common objectives. Through the tenders, every citizen can get involved in the collective effort to achieve society's objectives. Citizens are incentivized to participate in the areas and objectives that they are most interested in and to do so to the extent they wish to get involved. In a Democratic Objectivecracy, all citizens participate to choose the objectives of their society and then each one separately decides how much they want to get involved in the functioning of their society and the effort to achieve the objectives of the society, proposing projects and collective contracts through tenders. Each citizen participates to the extent in which he wants to participate and in what he wishes to participate.

In a Democratic Objectivecracy, collective contracts are always available for public scrutiny, and if enough citizens join, they can veto or modify a collective contract. Citizens always have the power to veto. There will be collective contracts that apply to all citizens and others that apply only to citizens who wish to carry out specific actions such as driving, starting a business, exploiting some natural resource, etc.

For example: A citizen who wants to drive a car needs to sign the collective contract that gives him the right to drive cars and make use of the collective infrastructure, and which commits him to follow certain traffic regulations and guidelines and even make certain payments for the maintenance of public infrastructure or to offset his carbon footprint.

All citizens have full access to all the information on the operation of administrations, audits and tenders. They also have the option to join together and, after reaching a required percentage of the population, they can modify or veto a collective contract, a project, or a verdict from a jury.

Citizens at all times have the authority to report and to warrant an audit of another citizen, a private entity, a member of an assembly, or a tenderer if he has proof they are failing to comply with a collective or a private contract.

Each society must develop the way in which it determines whether a person is a citizen or not. This decision can also be made using democracy by average, every election cycle each individual citizen proposes the age of adulthood and citizenship and the amount of time a migrant has to live inside a society to be considered a citizen. The individual proposals of all citizens are averaged to obtain the age of adulthood and citizenship.

For example:
All people who have lived at least 18 years in the society have the right to be citizens.

Upon reaching the age of Adulthood, each individual is given the option to sign a collective contract in which the individual, in exchange for the rights and benefits offered by being a member of the society, accepts that their society is organized according to the Democratic Objectivecracy, and gives administrators the power to sign collective contracts on their behalf.

If an individual does not wish to sign the collective contract, she has the following options:

1) Sign a partial contract that allows her to live in the territory controlled by the society, but without the right to use infrastructure, services, or to be benefited by any action of the social contract; In addition, the partial contract gives her the right to live in the territorial limits or restricts certain actions that could threaten the safety of other members of society.

2)

   a) The person will not be able to use public infrastructure such as streets, public spaces, water and drainage services, electricity, etc. Or, if she wishes to use them, she will have to pay a different fee to the society in order to use the infrastructure they built through their joint effort.

   b) The person cannot tender or be selected as a jury or assembly member.

   c) The person can only sue others according to the terms of the partial contract they signed.

   d) Depending on the economic arrangement of the society, the right to participate in the economy of the society can be limited or removed.

   e) Depending on the arrangement of each society, but the person may lose the right to sell or undertake projects or companies with other members of the society or whose products affect the society.

2) The person has the option of not signing any contract and leaving the territory administered by the society. The person has a passport but does not have legal protection and the right to participate within the society. That is, with limited citizenship. This limited citizenship must restrict the legal rights of the citizen.

If the person does not wish to sign the collective contracts, that is, to participate in the society she has the right to do so, but she cannot be the beneficiary of anything that happens or occurs within the society, nor will he be protected by the society.

The freedom to opt out is difficult to conceive for individual people living in a city, but it paves the way for groups of people to organize and develop a new independent society. It is important to have this option available because this will pave the way for peaceful separatist movements. Only if the society presents a peaceful means for dissent and separation will its citizens maintain their freedom. By presenting a peaceful process to separate and divide society, the oppression and violence needed to maintain unification and control in a society whose members do not want to be part of said society will be avoided. Only if the members of the society that do not want to be part of that particular society have a peaceful process through which they can opt out of the society will they be able to know themselves to be free, and be able to achieve the goal of separating from the society without viewing the society they are separating from as oppressive and an enemy whom they have to fight with violence. If a society can separate or unite through a free and peaceful process, the members of the new, different societies can be part of a confederation of independent societies. These separations can be as simple as a municipality breaking up into two or three different municipalities, each with their own objectives and democratic processes, but together they can form a confederation of municipalities to establish common objectives and joint projects to achieve those objectives. This system of social organization permits the fragmentation of society into small units where citizens have common objectives, and the unification of small units with common objectives to form confederations.

This gives small communities the tools not to sign the collective agreement of a larger society and to develop their own society. Perhaps in a small territory in the countryside within the territory managed by a larger society, some people decide not to sign the collective contract and create a small independent society. Or all members of a town or city refuse to sign the collective contract with another larger society like a country and thus gain independence from this larger society and constitute their own society. The important thing is that nobody can be forced to be part of a society and that there are ways and methods to create independent societies.

Minors

When a citizen has a child, he signs a contract with the other citizens of the society in which he stipulates that he is responsible for providing his child with all the basic things necessary for their survival and development and that he can be held accountable if the child breaches any collective contract. The child of the citizen is entitled to all the benefits of being a citizen minus the possibility of choosing society's objectives and they cannot be selected to be jurors or assembly members. Parents and citizens hold all the duties and responsibility for the actions of their children. When a child reaches adulthood, they are given the option to sign the full or partial collective agreement or to leave the society. Even minors can present tenders, although they cannot be members of juries, assemblies, or committees.

Immigrants or Tourists

Upon entering the territory controlled by a society, an immigrant or tourist must sign a contract with all their citizens submitting to the fulfillment of collective contracts but without having some of the rights that they provide, such as the right to choose the objectives of the society, to tender, or to be a member of an assembly or jury.

Each society must develop its own form of social organization including who is a citizen, what happens to those who do not want to sign the social contract, and what happens to immigrants, how long it will take and what they have to do in order for them to become citizens. The above are just examples and recommendations.

CHAPTER 10

Why this Social Structure?

Why have Citizens' Assemblies?

Not all citizens can be experts in everything. Not all of us can dedicate the time necessary to investigate, evaluate, debate, discern, and deliberate on all issues that affect our lives and the lives of the other members of the society.

Having Assemblies allows a group of people to dedicate 100% of their working time and effort to analyzing society's problems, situation, objectives, and the tenders proposed by the other citizens; to analyzing proposals, to listening and learning from experts and proponents on the topics they evaluate; to deliberating, debating and reaching agreement on possible solutions to problems, and on possible routes to achieving society's objectives; to making informed and conscious decisions.

When an Assembly is formed, the Assembly members are responsible for the outcomes and consequences of their decisions, while in a direct democracy that responsibility is diluted. The responsibility the members of the Assemblies have and the accountability they are subject to, will incentivize them to evaluate and decide with as much information and deliberation as possible.

Why empower citizens to veto the decisions of Assemblies?

If citizens have to vote to approve every legislation or proposal, then the system will be a direct democracy, in which case the problems we have already observed about direct democracy will emerge. For example, the citizens will have to spend too much time deliberating and making decisions about public life, even the parts of public life they are not interested in or have no stake in. But if citizens cannot get involved in anything, then some of the decisions of the Assemblies may seem illegitimate and citizens may feel or be oppressed. Or even worse, if there is no way for citizens to limit the power of Assemblies, they could begin to act contrary to the objectives of society and oppressively towards the citizens. If citizens do not have to approve the decisions of the Assemblies, but have the faculty to veto their decisions, the citizens maintain power and know that even if they do not have to be involved in everything, at the moment when they strongly disagree with a decision taken by an Assembly, they can organize to veto that decision. The responsibility for the proposals lies with the Assemblies and tenderers, but the power lies in all the citizens.

One of the purposes of the Democratic Objectivecracy is the unification of society under common objectives. If an action or decision of an Assembly is divisive or a part of the society considers itself to be oppressed by said decision, they can open a complaint and have available channels to veto a project or collective contract and to remove assembly members, or all the members of an assembly. This system is designed so that no one is or feels oppressed.

Why empower citizens to have the option to remove the Assemblies?

Assemblies have responsibility, but power is in the hands of citizens. If citizens have the means to change the members of the Assemblies, then the members of the Assemblies are responsible but not rulers, and oppression of citizens becomes practically impossible.

If citizens do not have confidence in the Assemblies, then the decisions of the Assemblies have no legitimacy over them. Citizens must have the power to remove members of Assemblies in order for their decisions to be considered democratic and legitimate. Citizens must have the power to remove members of Assemblies in order for every citizen to know that collective contracts and projects are not an imposition on him, but part of the democratic process in which he, together with all members of the society, decides and has control over the direction of their society.

On the other hand, if citizens are sure that there are no groups with power that are manipulating them or that are taking advantage of them, they will know that there is no specific group guilty if they have an unfavorable situation, and therefore they will know and feel responsible for their own destiny. Giving citizens the power to veto Assembly decisions and the power to demand that members of Assemblies be changed makes citizens ultimately responsible for the decisions of the members of the Assemblies.

Why have an assembly of Administrators?

The Assembly of Administrators is responsible for making decisions. It is necessary to have a group of people who dedicate 100% of their working hours to researching, deliberating, debating, listening to experts, etc. to make the best possible decisions according to the objectives of the society. Administrators do not have vertical authority, but they do have part of the responsibility for achieving the objectives of the society.

Why have an Assembly of Auditors?

The Assembly of Auditors is responsible for ensuring that there is no corruption and that Administrators and tenderers are effective and efficient. The Auditors are also in charge of the trials. The Assembly of Auditors ensures that there will be accountability in social organization.

Citizens cannot be expected to spend 100% of their time evaluating and analyzing what Administrators and tenderers do. It is necessary that a group of citizens have the responsibility to ensure that there is no corruption and that Administrators and tenderers fulfill their responsibilities, the projections of their tenders, and adhere to the objectives of society.

Why are all actions done through tenders?

If the Assemblies make decisions and choose, but do not execute, then their power is limited and the power to act and realize society's objectives is in the hands of the citizens. This means that the Assemblies will not have power to oppress citizens as they have no power to execute actions.

If citizens execute the actions and are monitored, evaluated, and judged by the Assembly of Auditors, and citizens can ask to stop an action, a project, or a collective contract by uniting a part of the population against it, then power is in the hands of citizens and even those who execute have no power over the other citizens. The tenderers execute projects, then the Auditors evaluate the results of these projects according to the objectives of the whole society and the specific, projected results presented during the tender. Furthermore, a project or collective contract can be stopped or vetoed by the citizens. This ensures that large amounts of power are not concentrated in a few hands and protects society from corrupt and oppressive actions.

Furthermore, if citizens are in charge of achieving the objectives of the society, a participatory democracy is generated in which the participation of the citizen is not reduced to an election one day every given amount of years or to veto and stop the actions of the Assemblies. Rather, the citizen is encouraged to participate, to propose, to make their society really their own and to achieve their objectives. By receiving financing from the society, citizens are encouraged to participate even more. By having to compete with other tenderers, the citizen has to strive to carry out the best possible project to achieve the objectives of the society and is efficient in its cost-benefit ratio. When audited, tenderers must ensure that their actions are what they promised they would be and that the results are in accordance with the objectives of society and their projections.

Tenders of this type avoid oppression, distribute power among many, promote and stimulate citizen participation, promote efficiency, and ensure that society's actions adhere to its objectives.

In addition, tenders allow citizens to become involved in the actions of their community, allowing and promoting their development within their society through social projects.

Under this system, all citizens choose the objectives of their society and compete with each other to work to achieve these objectives. Society is in the hands of the citizens.

How does the division of powers work in this new society?

The division of powers in this new social structure is designed to eliminate the possibility of corruption and oppression. It manages to do so by granting the administrators the power to approve or disapprove project or contract proposals but not giving them the opportunity to propose or execute projects themselves. On the other hand, Auditors have the power to evaluate and judge the decision-making process and the result of the approved projects, but they do not have the power to approve, propose, or execute projects themselves. Citizens can propose and execute projects and contracts, and they can evaluate, judge, and veto the decision-making processes and the results of contracts and projects, but they cannot approve and decide between the projects proposed by other citizens.

The citizens can propose through tenders and evaluate and judge the decision-making process of the Assemblies and the results of the executed tenders. The Administrator Assemblies can choose among the tenders proposed by the citizens, but they can't propose nor can they execute tenders. The Auditor's Assembly can evaluate and judge the Administrators Assembly and the selected tenders and projects that are being executed by the citizens, but they can't propose or execute projects, nor can they decide from among the projects proposed by the citizens to the Administrators. Power is distributed in such a way as to generate an effective organization and to eliminate the possibility of oppression.

What does the Democratic Objectivecracy and the new social structure achieve?

The Democratic Objectivecracy with the new social structure ensures that society is organized in a truly democratic and efficient way. The combination of the different types of democracy ensures that each citizen has the right to choose the reason why he is part of the society, what he looks for in the society, and the circumstances in which he wants to live; that each citizen can identify some of his objectives in the objectives of the society; that society unites to achieve its common objectives; that all citizens retain power over those who make decisions and over those who carry out actions that affect all members of society; that all the decisions of society are made to achieve specific objectives and are evaluated and judged according to these objectives; that all citizens can participate in proposing actions, projects, and collective contracts to achieve the society's objectives; that the actions of the society to achieve its objectives are effective because the tenderers have to compete against other proposals to achieve the same objectives and are evaluated according to their projected results.

The Democratic Objectivecracy and the new social structure manage to form a truly democratic society where citizens know themselves to be the owners of their own destiny, where they are incentivized to participate, propose, and act, and where they are united for common objectives.

The Democratic Objectivecracy and the new social structure manage to organize a society in which citizens will not be or feel oppressed. A society that is practically impossible to corrupt and from which it is impossible for a dictator to emerge.

Achievements of the new system:

1. Through the Democracy Objectivecracy, every citizen is part of the process of determining their society's objectives. There are no winners and losers because the decisions that the citizen has to take are not binary, their individual choices are averaged, and therefore everyone can identify part of their objectives in the common objectives of the whole society; everyone will know that they were not left out, every single person carries the same weight and power when deciding their society's objectives.

2. Having citizen assemblies where the members are selected by lottery ensures that there are no powerful groups or oligarchies controlling and manipulating the citizenry, and at the same time it allows a group of citizens to dedicate all their working time, effort, and talent to the deliberation and decision-making process, and it makes the Assembly members responsible for the results of the decisions they make.

3. Through tenders, a participatory democracy is generated where all citizens have the opportunity to participate in issues of their interest.

4. The Assembly of Auditors ensures that all the decisions and actions of the Assembly of Administrators and tenderers work according to the objectives and to achieve the projected results.

5. Citizens have the power to veto decisions and projects and to remove members of Assemblies if they do not trust them, ensuring that power and responsibility are ultimately in the hands of citizens.

What do you think of the elimination of the structure most governments use right now? Of the elimination of the legislative, executive, and judicial branches of government? What do you think of giving citizens the opportunity and responsibility to do all the actions needed to achieve society's objectives through tenders? Do you think that citizens can really take charge of the organization and actions needed to develop a functioning society? Do you think that this system encourages citizen participation? What do you think of the Assembly of Administrators and the work that they have to do? What do you think of the Assembly of Auditors and the work that they have to do? Do you think Auditors can really keep Administrators and tenderers in check? Do you think that tenders, collective contracts, and projects can really be measured, evaluated, and judged according to the objectives the members of society choose? What do you think of changing the concept of law to collective contracts? Do you think this system would really be a democracy? Do you think that in this system the power is held by the citizens? Do you think that in this system citizens are more free than in the current one? Do you think that this system could give more freedoms than the ones it restricts from citizens? Can you think of any way that this system could be improved? Do you think there could be a better system? Would you like to participate in such a system? Would you like to put together projects and tenders to achieve society's objectives? Do you think this new system will be efficient in achieving society's objectives? What would you improve? What would you change? What part don't you consider necessary? Do you think something else is necessary? More or less structure? More hierarchy? What do you like and dislike about this way of organizing society? How would you improve it?

CHAPTER 11

Democratic Selection Process

Each society must seek the most democratic and optimal way to select the objectives of the society the members of the Assemblies and every other decision they have to make. Each society must deliberate on the length of the administrative cycles, deciding how often new objectives are chosen and new members are selected for the Assemblies.

Democratically-Elected Objectives

The election of objectives can be made through the average system previously explained. Each citizen generates a scale of positive objectives and a scale of negative objectives. To each objective, he assigns a percentage of the 100 points available to him according to the importance he considers the objective to have. The objective scales of all members of the society are averaged to obtain the objective scale of the entire society.

There are objectives and issues that cannot be averaged and that can be very polarizing in society. In this case, the Administrative Committee must identify said polarizing objectives and issues that cannot be averaged, remove them from the usual election system, and set up a specific committee for the resolution of said conflict. The operation of said committee will be specified later.

The fact that each citizen develops his own scale of objectives does not mean that there can be no proselytizing, campaigning, public discussion, or debate on the objectives of society. In fact, the ideal is that members of society are constantly deliberating and debating the objectives of their society. However, in order to protect individuals and society from being manipulated, I recommend establishing certain requirements and certain regulations for debating and proselytizing.

For example:

1. Society will always allow and encourage discussion and debate about objectives and ideas.

2. Society will promote debate among its citizens. Organizing debates in schools, universities, public spaces, neighborhoods, clubs, and in all possible types of media. If a person wants to promote an objective, he must do so through discussion and debate.

3. No opinion can be censored or limited by society; everything will always be subject to discussion and debate.

4. Proselytizing does not occur through advertising campaigns or slogan advertising, but through debate. Advertising and paid slogans are prohibited.

5. It is strictly forbidden for companies or private entities to proselytize. The only accepted proselytizing is that carried out through debate between individuals. Companies or private entities can organize debates and finance the distribution of debates by the different media; but if there is a specific interest of the group or the company organizing or distributing the debate it has to be disclosed at the beginning and at the end of the debate. If the people organizing and promoting a debate have a specific agenda or are benefited by a specific objective or idea, they have to disclose this information so that the viewer can take it into account.

For example, if a food company finances a debate, at the beginning and at the end of the debate it has to specify who finances the debate and that they have a particular interest in choosing certain objectives.

6.   If a citizen becomes a "champion", or "leader" of a cause or objective, he will have to publicly state his reasons for promoting that objective and the possible benefits that he, his company, family, or acquaintances can obtain from the election of said objective. Auditors have the right to inquire about the person to ensure that the citizen promoting the objective is being honest with their declaration of intent. In case there is a discrepancy between the declared interests and the benefits that said "Leader" or "Champion" of a cause or objective, said discrepancy will be made public and said citizen will be sanctioned with a punishment corresponding to the crime of attempted manipulation of citizenship.

This means that payment to people, celebrities, influencers, etc. to adopt and promote an objective is prohibited. A person, group, or company cannot pay a person to promote an objective. Each person can promote the objectives they want but cannot receive money for adopting positions and promoting objectives.

Selection by lot of members of the Assemblies:

The selection of the members of the Assemblies of Administrators, Auditors, and juries is done by the process of sortition democracy. Because, although the Objectivecracy establishes the objectives of society which will be the metrics and parameters to evaluate and judge the actions of the Assemblies, if the members of the Assemblies are chosen through elections, the result will be the creation of a political class, of political proselytism and the government of an oligarchy that does not necessarily respond to the objectives of society. Against voting to elect the members of the committees, we can apply all the criticism and arguments we used against electoral representative democracy.

There are many ways in which democracy by lottery can be used to select the citizens to form the Assemblies. I present only two options:

1.   Selection by lottery among all citizens

The members of the Assemblies will be selected from all citizens of legal age. The selected citizens will be remunerated a salary and benefits that the citizens themselves choose when they are electing their objectives. To decide the salaries and benefits of the members of the assemblies, citizens can use democracy by average.

For example, every election cycle, the citizens can answer the following questions:

What is the monthly wages you want the Assembly members to have? How many hours a week do you want them to work on the Assembly matters?

The answer each citizen gives to these questions is averaged to obtain the decision of the whole of society. If the salary is too low, many citizens will not want to participate; if the salary is too high the burden of the Assemblies might be too much for the society to finance. Every society has to evaluate and debate these topics.

Each society must also evaluate, debate, and decide how to handle the issue of the personal projects of those who will be members of the Assemblies.

It is very important that the citizens selected to be members of the Assemblies have the right to withdraw and to decide not to participate. The selection is by lottery, but participation is not mandatory. It is voluntary.

1.   Selection by lottery and social service

The members of a society may stipulate that providing social service is one of the requirements to belong to the society. Social service is time and effort that each citizen provides to the service of society. For projects that lead society to achieve its objectives, it is time dedicated exclusively to the benefit of society. This is similar to a tax, but instead of asking citizens to dedicate their time and effort to work to earn money and then to give part of that money to the public treasury, in this case, citizens ask one another to give part of their time and effort directly to working to achieve the society's objectives. This is similar to the draft, but instead of requiring citizens to fight wars, citizens are required to give social service. Citizens themselves will decide how much time each citizen has to give for service to the whole society. This is decided by all members of the society as a whole through the average democracy system.

For example:
The society can be separated by age groups and the members of the society can decide how much time they think that the members of each age group should dedicate to the service of the society.

0 - 12 years = 0 time of social service
13 - 17 years = 1 month per year of social service
18 - 22 years = 3 days a month of social service
23 - 26 years = 1 year of social service
26 - 60 years = 1 month per year of social service
61 - 70 years = 1 year of social service
71 - onward = time of voluntary social service

The time that each citizen thinks that citizens of each age group should dedicate to social projects is averaged with that proposed by absolutely all citizens to obtain the average. This average becomes the time required for each citizen to dedicate to social work.

All citizens who are working in their social service time will be paid the same for their time, regardless of their economic level and what type of social service they perform. Individuals cannot decide what kind of social service they will do. Citizens who submit tenders to achieve society's objectives can request for financial resources and for people of different ages or with different skills and knowledge to work on their projects to achieve a social objective.

For example, some of the people who have to give time for social service can be used to set up a body of citizen guards that patrol the streets dedicating their time and full attention to helping other citizens, to making complaints, obtaining evidence of crimes and administrative offenses and following up on complaints from other citizens.

The time for social service can also be used to develop reforestation projects, cleaning of city areas, or any other project proposed by tendering citizens and approved by the Administrators' Assembly.

While some citizens dedicate their time to tendered projects or to being citizen guards, other citizens can be selected by lot to be members of the Assemblies. This implies that all citizens dedicate the same amount of time to the service of society, and that some of these citizens are selected by lottery to be part of the assemblies of Administrators and Auditors. This will allow all citizens to have the same amount of opportunities and freedoms to pursue their personal projects and goals and that everyone will have to dedicate the same time to social service, be it as part of an Assembly or as part of another project.

For example, all young people between 23 and 26 years old and adults between 60 and 70 years old can be asked to provide a year of social service and, using democracy by lottery, some can be selected to be part of the Assemblies of Auditors and Administrators. Citizens between the ages of 26 and 60 can be asked for a month each year or a couple of days each month for social service. Within these groups of citizens that have to give their social service, the Assembly members will be selected by lot. The citizens chosen by lot who are between the age of 23 and 26 and those who are between the age of 60 and 70 will dedicate their social service year to be 100% dedicated to the work of the Assemblies, while those selected by lot who are between 26 and 60 will dedicate only the amount of time stipulated of social service for their ages. With this in mind, a dynamic could be generated in which those who are 100% dedicated do the greatest amount of research and work and they present their conclusions and proposals to those who only dedicate a small part of their time and together they deliberate and make the final decision.

This process will allow citizens to plan their life, taking into account the time they will have to dedicate to their society, and therefore their personal projects will not be interrupted if they are selected by lottery to be part of an Assembly since all citizens have to provide the same time of social service. The difference would be that some dedicate their service to work on specific projects and others will be members of the Assemblies.

Collaboration between members of different generations and different parts of society to form Assemblies, work on tenders, and as citizen guards will accustom members of society to collaborating with each other, communicating and organizing. This will strengthen social cohesion and society's capacity to respond to crises.

On the other hand, asking those under 25 for one year of social service may justify certain benefits such as free university education; and asking those over 60 years of age to serve society for some time may justify the entire society paying for their pensions. Social service in this way does not become an obligation that society imposes on the citizen but a service that society asks of the citizen and in return it provides certain benefits.

The constant collaboration between the two generations will also help balance the innovative impulses of young people with the natural desire for stability for retirees who will depend entirely on the stable functioning of society to receive their pension. The knowledge, motivations and interests of both generations will complement each other in the decision-making process there will always be people with experience who have worked for the development of the current circumstances and the current world affairs, and there will always be people present who will want to develop their own future, their own circumstances, and to evolve their society.

Furthermore, having all members of the society dedicate the same amount of time to social service, and choosing the members of the Assemblies among the people that have to do social service will be the fairest way to select assembly members by lot because every citizen will have to give the same amount of time in his life to do social service. If the assembly members are selected from among the general public, then the society will be asking some people to interrupt their personal projects and life to give their time and effort to be part of the democratic process. But if every single person has to give the same amount of time to social service, people can plan their life beforehand, taking into account the time they have to dedicate to social service. It is true that some people will not want to give part of their time for social service, just as some people will want the society to charge zero taxes. These people can vote for zero taxes and zero time for social service, and by doing so, they will lower the amount of taxes and social service everyone has to give to achieve the society's objectives. These people can also decide to opt out of the society and develop a separate society that works any way they want it to work. The Democratic Objetivcracy does ask for its citizens' attention, work, and effort. In return, it gives them power, the possibility of self-determination, and it expands their freedoms, opportunities and possibilities. It let's them choose the benefits the society will give them, it protects them from abuses of power, from oppression and exploitation, and it generates the possibility of carrying out small and large-scale projects to achieve the citizens' common objectives. A society where no one either pays taxes or dedicates time and effort to the social organization and the common objectives of the society is a society without organization where everyone will be left to fend for themselves and where people with power will be able to use it to oppress or exploit people with less power. Time and resources are needed to develop a society that will expand the freedoms and opportunities of its members and that will protect them from oppression and exploitation.

Recommendations:

It is very important that citizens selected to be members of the assemblies have the right to withdraw and not participate. Selection is by lottery, but participation is not mandatory, it is voluntary.

To protect the system from corruption and to increase the possibilities of the participation of different members of society, it is recommended that:

1) Citizens convicted or pending trials in cases of corruption or defrauding society or certain other crimes are excluded from the selection process.

2) The immediate relatives of citizens participating in the Assemblies of the cycle that is about to end are excluded for a period of time.

3) The father, mother, siblings, and children of a person who participates in an Assembly is excluded from the selection process for the next Assembly. This will help the Assemblies be more diverse and there will be more possibilities for all members of society to have first or second-hand knowledge of the assembly process.

Once the members of the Assemblies have been selected, their names are published and their labor relations, legal situation, financial situation, resume, kinship, and friendship are made public. Citizens will have the right to veto a member of the Assemblies if they collect enough signatures. Citizens who are randomly selected, are not vetoed by citizens, and who do not recuse themselves, will be the members of the Assemblies.

Once the Assemblies are established, the members will hire teams of consultants and researchers to help them gather information and understand the various social issues that come into play on the objective scale. These hires must be justified and the information on who these consulting teams are will be public and subject to public scrutiny. Citizens may veto a team of consultants or sue a committee member for nepotism or misuse of their resources.

Percentages of citizens necessary to veto decisions or revoke tenders

In order for citizens to maintain their sovereignty at all times, they themselves have to decide the percentage of citizens necessary to veto or modify a decision of an Assembly, a collective contract or a tendered project. What percentage of citizens is necessary to request that all members of an Assembly be fired and that a new Assembly be formed? What percentage of non-compliance with the projected results of the tenders is necessary to stop a project or a collective agreement; and what is the percentage of noncompliance with projected results that would trigger a fraud investigation of tenderers?

These decisions can also be made using Average Democracy. Each citizen proposes the percentage they think is correct for each question, and the responses of all citizens are averaged.

For example:

What is the percentage of citizens required to veto or modify a decision of an Assembly, a collective agreement, or a project?

	Citizen 1	Citizen 2	Citizen 3	Citizen 4	Total
Percentage of citizens	20%	50%	60%	10%	35%

What percentage of citizens is necessary to request that all members of an Assembly be fired and that a new Assembly be formed?

	Citizen 1	Citizen 2	Citizen 3	Citizen 4	Total
Percentage of citizens	40%	60%	70%	20%	47.5%

What percentage of non-compliance with the projected results of the tenders is necessary to stop a project or a collective contract?

	Citizen 1	Citizen 2	Citizen 3	Citizen 4	Total
Percentage of non-compliance with results	30%	35%	40%	20%	31.25%

What percentage of non-compliance with the projected results is necessary to automatically trigger a fraud investigation of tenderers?

	Citizen 1	Citizen 2	Citizen 3	Citizen 4	Total
Percentage of non-compliance with projections	40%	50%	60%	40%	47.5%

Do you think that the election of Assemblies by lottery is a democratic process and would allow power to remain in the hands of citizens? Do you think these processes would eliminate the propensity of systems to be corrupted? What do you think of proselytizing through debates? Do you think there would be ways to improve these electoral systems to make them more democratic and more participatory? Do you think it is a good idea for the citizens themselves to decide how many of them have to disagree with the decisions in order to veto them? Do you think it will be a good idea if all members of society have to give some of their time for social service? What do you think of the proposal to select younger and older people to form the main body of the Assemblies? How can you improve the elections, selections, and campaigns?

Non-averaging and polarizing objectives of society.

Before each election, a special committee within the Administrative Assembly is selected by lot to evaluate public debates to identify whether there are highly divisive and polarizing issues that cannot be averaged; objectives whose average would generate division, dissatisfaction, and social discontent. The committee presents these issues to the entire Assembly of Administrators who have to assess whether the issue is truly polarizing or not. If the entire Assembly of Administrators concludes that the topic is polarizing and not able to be averaged, it presents this topic and their reasoning to the citizens. Citizens then face a referendum where they can decide whether to leave the issue to be decided through the regular average election of the objectives, or to remove the issue from the electoral cycle.

These topics will be dealt with outside the objective scale average electoral system because there is no way to average or find a middle ground on such a topic. To solve these issues, an assembly of citizens is generated with the specific task of finding a solution to the polarization and the specific issue that society is facing. The members of the Assembly are chosen by lot. This Assembly has the objective of obtaining a proposal for a collective contract or project that solves the problem and generates the greatest possible social cohesion.

The members of the Assembly will deliberate, debate among themselves, and listen to the arguments of citizens, proponents of the topic, or specialists whom they think can contribute to their deliberations. There will also be a period in which members of the general public can present proposals for solutions to the Assembly. The Assembly deliberates internally and will seek to establish a plan, a collective contract, or an action that solves the problem and generates social cohesion.

Said Assembly will generate a recommendation that will be presented with its due justification to be evaluated by the Assembly of Administrators, Auditors and citizens in general; either of the two assemblies or citizens can veto the resolution.

If neither of the assemblies nor the citizens, veto the recommendation of the Assembly that works on the subject, then this Assembly on behalf of the citizens signs the collective contract with the resolutions on the subject.

If the citizens veto the resolution, the Assembly will deliberate again, receiving citizens, proponents of an objective, and experts who will give arguments for one side or the other. The Assembly will again seek a resolution satisfactory to all and will publish it. If the Assembly repeats the process three times and does not obtain the approval of the citizens, half of the Assembly is selected by lot and leaves the Assembly, the other half remains and new members selected by lot from the population are added. This process is repeated until a proposal is approved by the citizens.

What do you think? Do you think it is worth separating the most polarizing and divisive issues from the process by which the objectives of society are chosen? Do you think that if we unite people in the search for a solution to polarizing problems, a satisfactory proposal can be generated? Do you think that we could really find answers to the problems that divide society the most in this way?

____

____

____

____

Crisis and stations that need fast responses

Every society has moments in its history where it faces unprecedented crises and problems. If the social structure does not have the mechanisms to face these crises and can only work for its objectives selected in advance, then it will hardly be able to survive. In order to ensure the survival of the society, the Assembly of Administrators, Auditors, or a substantial number of citizens can declare an emergency or crisis.

Once a crisis is declared, the steps to resolve it are:

1) Administrators develop collective emergency contracts that will only work for a limited period. These emergency collective agreements are intended to generate a rapid first response to the crisis.

2) Administrators suspend projects that have low percentage points on the objective scale, or that are not considered essential for the functioning of society and direct the efforts of those projects and their budgets to resolve the crisis.

3) Administrators modify the objectives of projects that have organization, knowledge, or resources that can be used to face the crisis. Administrators can only modify the objectives of the projects while the tenderers have to modify their actions and projects to achieve the new objectives; or Administrators can modify the objectives and request certain specific actions.

For example, a security guard agency may have a tender to patrol the streets of a city. Administrators can change the tender to ask this agency, during the crisis, to bring food directly to the homes of all citizens.

1) Administrators communicate to the public what the crisis is, why they think the crisis developed, and what actions they are taking to solve it. They can also open a tender to receive proposals for contracts and projects that help solve the crisis.

2) Citizens can vote to deny that it is a crisis and to stop any action on the issue. Citizens can vote to approve that it is a crisis, but not to approve the immediate actions that Administrators are taking. When citizens approve of the crisis, but not the decisions of the Administrators, the Administrators have to quickly modify their response while waiting for tender proposals.

3) Citizens and private entities can apply to the tender with projects to solve the problem or the crisis.

4) The crisis is resolved by the actions and decisions that the administrators take when declaring it and the projects that citizens launch through tenders.

5) If the crisis is big enough, administrators can propose a change in society's objectives, putting the resolution of the crisis as a primary objective. Citizens can veto this proposal from Administrators

and call for an express election of objectives. In this scenario, all citizens re-choose their objectives for the duration of the emergency. It is very important that these elections can be organized quickly and that all citizens have means to choose their objectives.

6) Administrators open tenders to receive projects aimed at solving the crisis. Initial decisions of Administrators continue to operate until they receive and approve new tenders.

For example: Society is affected by a drought that affects farmers, food supply, and food prices. The Administrators propose to spend funds that were initially intended to generate city infrastructure to develop an irrigation system or to import food and subsidize the recovery of farmers. They make these proposals available to citizens, who can accept the crisis and the solution, or accept the crisis and not the solution. The Administrators then open tenders for projects that can solve the problem. They review the projects. They choose some and present them again to the public who may or may not veto them.

Do you think that this would be a legitimate way to empower Administrators to act with discretion in the event of a crisis, but with sufficient mechanisms to limit their power should they try to abuse it? Do you think there is a better way for society to face crises without giving too much power to the Assemblies?

____

____

____

____

____

____

____

____

____

____

____

____

Oppressive elected objectives or projects.

The raison d'être of the Democratic Objectivecracy is to develop a free society made up of free human beings who, through collaboration expand their opportunities, possibilities, and freedoms. Therefore, if circumstances arise in which the society chooses an oppressive objective or that the Administrators choose an oppressive project for one or many of its members. Those who consider themselves oppressed have the opportunity to appeal to the auditors assembly, even if only one person is oppressed, they have the option to present their complaint and show how society is oppressing them. Upon receiving the complaint, the committee will have to assess whether it is really their freedom, or if it is a privilege or their power that is restrained by the objective or action. If the freedom requested by the individual in question does not threaten the freedom of the other members of society, if it does not threaten the freedom of society as a whole, and if the freedom in question is not a freedom that citizens have freely decided to dispense with to achieve an objective, if the auditors decide that there is reason to consider that the individual or group is being oppressed, then they will convene the formation of a new citizens' Assembly to assess the situation and develop a proposal. This proposal will then be presented to all citizens who will have the right to veto the proposal. The citizens who consider themselves oppressed also have the ability to veto the resolution if they consider it to be unsatisfactory.

If the Assembly of Auditors does not believe that the individual or group is being oppressed, the individual or group will have to gather a substantial number of signatures and, this time, appeal to the Assemblies of Administrators of past electoral cycles. If they still do not believe that a freedom is being violated, then they will have to gather a specific amount of support from the population. If they succeed, then the Assemblies, in turn, are forced to constitute a new Assembly to resolve the problem. The number of citizens supported should be decided using the process of Democracy by Average.

It must be remembered that there are certain freedoms that citizens renounce in order to participate in a society that has certain characteristics. By choosing the objectives of their society and accepting the Democratic Objectivecracy system, the individual accepts that their objectives are averaged with those of other citizens and therefore it is the average of all, not just their personal objectives, that establishes the circumstances and what is prohibited and permitted in the society. If, on average, all citizens seek to limit certain freedoms in order to have a society with certain characteristics, then the Assemblies will have to evaluate between the freedoms and the circumstances that society generates by being united and the specific freedoms that it limits. The Assembly will also have to consider whether the limitation of a freedom disproportionately affects a sector of the population and whether it really is oppressive or if it is a sacrifice voluntarily accepted by the rest of society to achieve its objectives.

Participation in the Democratic Objectivecracy must always be free; and mechanisms should always exist to ensure that those who feel oppressed can raise their voices and fight against their oppression in a peaceful and organized way. These mechanisms have to work in such a way that the individual does not feel crushed by the system but, at the same time, the system has to be stable. The system has to work for the whole society and not be overthrown by the first problem that arises. It is of the utmost importance that the members of a Democratic Objectivecracy are always on the lookout for improvements that they can make to the system, so that not only the objectives, circumstances, morals, justice, and society evolve, but alongside them, the system also evolves.

Do you think that it is possible to maintain stability in the system if any citizen can file a complaint against the system or the objectives of society? Do you think that this complaint mechanism can prevent society from becoming oppressive?

Electoral, transition and administration cycles.

Each society must seek the optimal duration of its electoral cycles and transition times between one administration and another. The duration of the electoral cycles must be reached by weighing the following considerations:

1) Social and system stability.

2) A long enough time to allow the implementation of projects that can attack problems in depth and from which results can be obtained in the short, medium, and long term.

3) A long enough time to allow the development and implementation of small and large scale projects that will help society to achieve its objectives.

4) A short enough time to allow the updating of the objective scale according to the evolution in the thinking and feeling of the citizens.

5) A short enough time to allow updating of the objective scale according to constantly changing circumstances.

6) A short enough time to allow the constant change of the members of the Assemblies so as not to put too much power in the hands of a few.

7) A long enough time to allow a gradual transition between administrations and tendered projects. The results of the elections should be implemented gradually and with the necessary

transition time to allow stability and the elaboration of concise projects.

If the members of the Assemblies are going to be chosen from the citizens who are going to give their social service, then it will be safe to assume that a single scale of objectives will guide society for the duration of various Assemblies. In this case, citizens will be asked how long they want the objectives they are choosing at the moment to govern their society; how much time they want every citizen to give to social service, and from what age groups they want the members of the assembly to be selected.

1)   How much time do you want the current objectives that are being chosen now to last?

________ years

2)   Divide the population into the age groups you deem fit and decide how much time each age group has to dedicate to social service:

Age group   Time for Social Service
___ to ___   _______________________
___ to ___   _______________________
___ to ___   _______________________
___ to ___   _______________________
___ to ___   _______________________
___ to ___   _______________________
___ to ___   _______________________
___ to ___   _______________________

3)   Among what age groups do you want the Assembly members to be chosen?

Age groups ____________

For example:

The citizens can decide that their objectives should guide society for the next seven years, and that the age groups from 23 to 26, and from 60 to 70 should give one year of their lives to social service and the citizens in the age group between 27 and 59 should give one month a year of social service. From the citizens in these three groups, the members of the Assemblies are chosen by lot. Those in the age groups between 23 and 26 and 60 and 70 will serve one year in the Assemblies and those in the age group between 27 and 59 will serve one month.

All of the Assembly members don't have to be changed at the same time; the changes can be gradual.

Let's put this in a more concrete example:

1) Day 1 of the electoral cycle:
   a) Objectives are chosen.

2) First four months of the electoral cycle:
   a) The objectives and the projects of the previous electoral cycle remain in place during the transition.

   b) One-third of the Assemblies, those who have already served one year, are replaced by new members. The other two-thirds of the Assembly members remain in place. The new Assembly members learn from those who were there previously and form their working teams.

   c) Citizens or private entities develop projects to achieve the new objectives that they will present in the tenders.

3) Next four months:
   a) The objectives and the projects of the previous electoral cycle remain in place during the transition.

   b) One-third of the Assemblies, those who have already served one year, are replaced by new members to the Assemblies. The other two-thirds of the Assembly members remain in their place. The new Assembly members learn from those who were there previously and they form their working teams.

c)   The Assembly of Administrators receives and evaluates the tenders.

d)   The Assembly members among the ages groups of 23 to 26 and 60 to 70 dedicate a whole year to serve in the Assemblies as they evaluate, deliberate, and decide what projects they want to approve, and they present their conclusions to the Assembly members in the age group of 26 and 59 that dedicate only one month a year to their work in the Assemblies. Together the three groups have to decide which projects they are going to approve and finance.

4) Next four months:
a)   The objectives and the projects of the previous electoral cycle remain in place during the transition.

b)   One-third of the Assemblies, those who have already served one year, are replaced by new members of the Assemblies. The other two-thirds of the Assembly members remain in their place. The new Assembly members learn from those who were there previously and they form their working teams.

c)   The Assembly of Administrators publish their conclusions for Auditors and citizens to evaluate, modify, or veto.

d)   Auditors can veto a project if they deem the selection process to have been corrupt or if they think the selected tender goes against one or more of the objectives of the society.

e)   The citizens can veto a project if they find it oppressive or corrupt, or they can work with the tenderer to modify a section of the project to better achieve society's objectives.

5) Second to seventh year of the cycle:
a)   The new objectives, tendered projects, and collective contracts are fully operational.

b) Auditors audit the implementation and results of the tendered projects and collective contracts.

c) One-third of the Assembly members keep changing every four months.

d) The Administrators collect taxes and keep selecting new tenders to replace the ones that did not comply with the percentage of projected results.

One of the advantages of this process is that a great amount of citizens participate in the assemblies and will have first hand knowledge on how they work and on the efficiency of the duration of the transition cycles. This means that when they vote to determine election and transition cycles and the duration of the assemblies, they will have first hand experience on these matters.

This is only one of many options available to structure the electoral cycle. I am sure that every society that implements the New system will develop an electoral cycle that will best fit their needs, characteristics, and circumstances.

If the electoral periods are too long, it would be unfair if those who are going to come of age during that period are not taken into account. Therefore, upon reaching the age of citizenship and signing their collective contract with the rest of society, each citizen has the right to present their scale of objectives. This implies that the scale of objectives will have some fluctuation throughout the electoral cycle. The projects already approved will be judged according to the scale of objectives under which they were approved and the projects that are evaluated throughout the administration will be evaluated and judged according to the objective scale at the time of their approval.

What do you think of the electoral cycles? Regardless of how long the transition time is, what do you think of the process? Do you think that a stable society will be achieved with these cycles? What do you think are the best process and the best transition times and administration cycles? What would your ideal electoral process look like?

Why select the members of the Assemblies by lottery?

Having an assembly of citizens elected by lottery allows us to eliminate the problem of having too much power in a few hands, to generate authority vertically, and to have groups with power or with certain interests that influence the elections or polarize the population through the elections.

There is no president of the Assembly or hierarchy inside the Assemblies. Societies will have to establish protocols to determine the committees, etc. but if they avoid a hierarchical system within an Assembly, then it will be very difficult for a powerful group or class to corrupt all members of the Assembly selected by lottery among the various demographics of the population.

If there is no vertical authority, then power is distributed horizontally and the possibility of generating an oppressive Assembly are reduced, because members of the Assembly were not part of a specific group and did not participate in political campaigns together to be able to be part of the Assembly. Furthermore, in the electoral representative democracy the president or governor can make a decision that will change people's lives. In the system we are proposing, no one person in the Assembly has that power. If no one has power over the others, then the mistakes of a single person from incompetence, ignorance, or corruption will not have devastating consequences on the entire population.

If there are no parties or elections, then the members of the Assemblies will deliberate according to their personal criteria and what they learn by investigating, listening to the opinions and proposals of the other committee members and the experts they hire to help them understand and judge the problems and the proposals at hand. However, their ideology and discretion is limited because they will be evaluated and judged according to the objectives of the society.

If the members of the Assembly are selected by lottery, the divisions and polarization generated by the election system are avoided. The system of selection by lottery avoids the polarization of society by politicians who seek power. It prevents one part of the population from being represented and the other from being ruled over, and that one part of the population is a winner and the other a loser. This is not a system that generates winners and losers.

If there are no elections, then people and groups with power cannot propose or support a candidate who will then work for these people with power and not for the citizens. The members of the Assemblies are selected by lottery, so nobody will know beforehand who will get selected. This person could be anyone, so no pre-election plans can be made to corrupt or manipulate the members of the Assembly. When selected by lottery, the members of the Assembly will most likely have different ideas and interests, so there will hardly be a prevailing ideological trend among the members of the Assembly that is not present in the population. But, even if there is a prevailing ideology among the members of an Assembly, the results of their decisions are judged according to the objectives of the whole society and the projected results of the projects and collective contracts. Even when holding a particular view on one subject, Assembly members are judged according to the objectives of the whole society, not their own. It would also be extremely difficult to corrupt all or most members of an Assembly because they come from different backgrounds and have no political career to consider, but even if a powerful group is successful in corrupting all the members of one Assembly, that Assembly will be evaluated and judged by another Assembly and by the citizens.

The Assembly system does not allow a single member of the Assemblies to be more important and gain more power than the others. The system of selection by lottery means that there will be no political campaigns to promote a candidate that could gain power thanks to the support of many citizens. In an Objectivecracy the objectives, ideas, ideals, and proposals of the citizens rule, not the objectives or ideas of the Assembly members or of those who make decisions. In this system, Assembly members have no executive or legislative power, they can only approve or disapprove proposals made by the citizens, and their decisions are evaluated by another Assembly and can be vetoed by the citizens. In this system, it is practically impossible for a person or a group to gain enough popularity or power to become dictators.

Assemblies elected by lottery eliminate the opportunities to corrupt decision makers; they eliminate the possibilities of a person making a decision that will benefit him and not the rest of society; they avoid the concentration of power in a single person, political parties, or interest groups that could legislate or execute according to their own interests; they eliminate the factions, polarization, and special interests that arise when legislators are party members; they eliminate the polarization generated in the political campaigns; they eliminate the possibility of the formation of oligarchies, political classes, or power groups that right now influence the politics of our society. The election by lottery of Assemblies also eliminates the possibility of a democracy becoming a dictatorship.

CHAPTER 12

Confederation of Democratic Objectivecracies

The system of Democratic Objectivecracies previously described, or other systems that apply the basic principles of the Objectivecracy and democracy, can be used to organize individually local societies that may, in turn, be part of an even larger society of Democratic Objectivecracies. The relationship between the societies generates a confederation and the way in which the confederation will organize itself is the same as the local Democratic Objectivecracy.

When an opportunity emerges to develop a partnership among societies, this is a society composed of more than one society. The individuals in each society choose the objectives for the confederation of societies. This means that they have a scale of objectives for their local society and one for the confederation of societies. The objectives that each individual chose for the confederation are averaged with the objectives of each person in the other societies to obtain the confederation's objective scale. According to its objectives, the confederation may undertake joint projects that involve members of all societies and financing of all societies to achieve objectives of a greater scale and greater impact than what a single society could undertake.

Perhaps a single society does not have enough resources to undertake a large-scale project to solve the environmental crisis or to face a pandemic, but a confederation of societies organized by the

Democratic Objectivecracy system might have the strength and resources to do so.

At the confederation level, the list of individual objectives are still averaged and not the list of objectives of the societies because if the objective scales of the societies are averaged, the objectives chosen by the members of a society with less population will have greater value than the objectives selected by a society with more citizens. To ensure complete democracy even at the confederate level, each individual objective list must have equal weight regardless of the society from which it comes.

The members of the Assemblies of the confederation will be selected in a similar way to the members of the Assemblies of the local society, with the difference that each society will be entitled to a number of representatives corresponding to the percentage of the population of the confederation that its society represents.

For example: in a confederation made up of ten societies, where one of these societies has 30% of the population of the entire confederation, this society is entitled to 30% of the members of the assemblies. Those members will be selected within each society in the same way as the other members of the administrations of each society, by lottery.

This will ensure that in a confederation of societies each human being in each society has the same rights, the same power, the same opportunity, and the same value.

A confederation of societies in turn can develop a confederation of confederations that scales the way the system works to a bigger confederation. The objective list each individual chooses for that particular partnership among confederations is averaged to obtain the scale of objectives of the confederation; The members of the assemblies are drawn by lot from among the confederations and each confederation is entitled to a number of members on the committee proportional to the individuals that make up that confederation.

By upscaling the system of societies to confederations and confederations of confederations, a global and even universal system can be generated for all humanity where all individuals live free from oppression and have the same rights, power, and opportunities to determine the objectives, terms, and conditions of their societies and the circumstances in which every human being lives.

Do you think this is a system that can be upscaled to a large scale? Do you think that it is possible to generate small communities that are organized through the Objectivecracy and confederations of many societies that continue to organize themselves through the system of the Democratic Objectivecracy? Do you think that by organizing in this way we have more to gain or lose? Do you think that a free global confederation of societies can be developed while maintaining individual freedom?

SECTION 5

RECOMMENDATIONS

By now, we have already explained what a Democratic Objectivecracy is, what an Average Democracy is, and how these principles could be applied to develop a new form of social organization and what its benefits are. However, these are only the basic principles to build a society, from here on other issues such as education and security have to be developed. Next, we will give some recommendations on the operation of a Democratic Objectivecracy. Keep in mind that these, like everything above, are just recommendations.

CHAPTER 1

Information and Transparency

In order for a Democratic Objectivecracy to function properly, complete transparency is necessary in all the actions, the decision-making process, and results and consequences of projects and collective contracts. For that reason, one of the main functions of the Auditors should be the collection of information and measurement of all possible aspects of the society and the results of each implemented tender. People can only be held accountable for the decisions they make if they have access to all the information available regarding the decision they have to take.

Citizens will be able to use the information to make decisions about what the priorities and objectives will be for the next electoral cycle and to objectively judge the results of the actions carried out according to the objectives they chose.

Complete transparency is one of the most important requirements for the existence of a true democracy. If there is a lack of transparency in a democracy, this means that the members of society are being denied information relevant to the decision they have to take, and the denial of information relevant for a decision implies the oppression and manipulation of the members of society, because denying information is forcing a person to decide without knowing, without taking into account information that could modify their decision. If certain information could change an opinion and a decision, then withholding that information is manipulation, because the withholder of information is preventing the ignorant person from choosing what they would choose if they had all the information available. This means that whoever withholds information is depriving the person of his right, in a democracy, to decide according to his own criteria. The withholder of information is deciding that the citizen should choose what he will choose if he doesn't have all the available or important information. Therefore, the withholder of information is manipulating the decision of the citizen and by doing so, he is oppression the citizen. A society that is not 100% transparent, completely and absolutely transparent, is not a democratic society. Members of society can only make decisions free of control, manipulation, and oppression if they have full access to all the information corresponding to the public life of the society.

It is not enough for society to allow the available information to be known. If a concrete effort is not made to obtain and collect all the information related to the public life of a society, individuals will not have access to relevant information to make decisions. The lack of information because it was hidden from the public eye, or because it was not collected, has the same harmful and oppressive effect on democratic society. Members of a society can only make truly free decisions if a society actively works to obtain all the information pertinent to public life and to distribute this information among its members.

In a society that is governed by the system of Democratic Objectivecracy, it is absolutely necessary to collect all possible information about the results and consequences of each collective contract and project of the society, so that in this way they can be evaluated and judged according to the objectives and their projected result. If there is no information or transparency, a society will not be able to judge public actions according to their objectives, and therefore it will not be a Democratic Objectivecracy.

If a person or a group withholds information because they think they are going to modify your point of view towards something that does not suit them when you decide without that information, are you being free or are you being manipulated? Do you think that it should be a crime, or considered manipulation, if administrations or governments hide information so that you do not change your points of view? How necessary do you think transparency and information is in a democracy?

____

____

____

____

____

____

____

____

____

____

____

____

____

Freedom of Expression

In a democratic objectivecracy, freedom of expression is not only necessary, but it should be encouraged. The society should also encourage debate and the questioning of the status quo by its members, so that they are always reviewing and evaluating the validity of their objectives and can modify them if their perspective on an objective changes.

Free expression and the debate of ideas and objectives is a requirement for the existence of a true democracy and, above all, of a true Democratic Objectivecracy. Only through debate can the reasons for choosing an objective maintain its validity and legitimacy. Only if the scale of objectives is constantly debated can the members of society be sure of and reaffirm the reasons why they have chosen certain objectives. Or they may realize that some objectives are no longer relevant or not necessary under current circumstances.

A Democratic Objectivecracy must not only allow debate and free expression but it must encourage debate and free expression. This promotion of debate will have the objective of keeping the entire system and the scale of objectives, in turn, legitimate; and by allowing the evolution of objectives, it ensures that members of society will never be or feel oppressed by an objective that they consider unnecessary, outdated, or irrelevant.

To find out more about freedom of expression and the benefits of debate, I recommend to the reader the book "On Liberty" by John Stuart Mill.

How do you think freedom of expression and debate could be promoted? Do you think there are ideas that should not be debated? Why?

CHAPTER 2

Education

A Democratic Objectivecracy will work most optimally when all its members are accustomed to employing democratic methods throughout their lives; when citizens are used to doing personal and group objective lists, and to developing and carrying out actions according to their objectives. Practical education is the best way to stimulate and promote the use of democracy and of objectivecracy in all areas of citizens' lives.

The objective of the Democratic Objectivecracy is not only to allow its members to be free and to develop without oppression, but to increase the possibilities, opportunities, and freedoms of its citizens; to achieve this it must ensure that all its members can have an education that promotes critical thinking, questioning authority and the status quo, debate, formation of personal criteria, and understanding of the functioning of the Democratic Objectivecracy system, at least a basic understanding of the natural world and of human history, and that they have the capacity to organize and collaborate together in teams and projects.

Furthermore, if a society governed by the system of Democratic Objectivecracy encourages and imparts analytical and critical education, it is ensuring that its members can choose their objectives through a proper deliberative process and that its members are capable of being part of an Assembly and making decisions that are not absurd, inefficient, or influenced by powerful manipulators.

A society that encourages and makes critical and practical education available to all its citizens, not only to its children but to all its members, is a society that ensures that they have competent citizens not only to choose their objectives and to be members of an Assembly, but to develop, propose, and carry out successful and efficient tendered projects to achieve society's objectives.

A society that encourages and makes education available to its citizens, not only to its children but to all its members, is a society that expands the freedom, possibilities, and opportunities of each human being, since their knowledge and critical education will empower them to strive, undertake and achieve personal and social projects.

To function properly, a Democratic Objectivecracy must promote a sense of personal and social responsibility, question the status quo, debate, the thirst for knowledge and argumentative logic, and constant collaboration and team work.

I recommend that the education systems in a Democratic Objectivecracy promote:

1)   The sense of personal and social responsibility and
     practice in the use of the democratic system.

It is essential that the members of a Democratic Objectivecracy understand that their personal future and that of their society is intertwined and in their own hands. Even though there are external forces, the same society being one of them, each citizen exercises an influence on his society and, in doing so, modifies his own circumstances and those of other citizens.

It is recommended that from a young age the formation of objective scales and decision-making with respect to said objectives is encouraged. It is also recommended that the democratic process be used in different ways throughout the education of citizens so that from childhood they get used to and feel empowered to speak out, participate, criticize, propose, organize, and act.

Depending on the size of the groups of children in the schools, activities employing different types of democracy can be carried out. These activities should be frequent and have real impacts on the lives of the students. In this way, they will live the democratic process with different systems throughout their lives, making the transition to use it at the political level as something natural.

For example: Children in a classroom may debate about the color they want to paint their classroom or about the place they want to go for a school trip and then choose through direct democracy. Some decisions about the operation of schools may be available to students who, in order to make decisions can use debates and the representative process by lottery and the veto power of the majority.

2)   Questioning the status quo.

To prevent obsolete dogmas from stagnating the progress and advancement of society, or from powerful groups generating an oppressive conception of reality for a section of society, all the citizens of a Democratic Objectivecracy should be accustomed to questioning the status quo. Only the objectives, structures, collective contracts, and projects that stand firm under questioning can justify their existence.

The following possibilities arise from questioning something:

a)   Through the questioning process an error or a fault is discovered and it is corrected or eliminated. Eliminating or correcting an error is, without a doubt, an action that we can consider positive for a democratic society.

b)   By responding to the question, the arguments in favor of the objective, idea, structure, etc. are reinforced and the fervor and resolution for said objective is strengthened.

c) By responding to the question, the members of a democracy see their democracy in operation and can be sure that the path taken by their society is the one they consider correct and legitimate with the knowledge they presently have and in the current circumstances.

It is also advisable to show citizens the advantages of stability and gradual changes and that change in a Democratic Objectocracy comes through questioning, debate, and the democratic process. It is recommended that citizens from childhood be encouraged to question the status quo and authority, and that those with authority get used to knowing that if they cannot justify their authority, they lack legitimacy.

3) Debates

Citizens of a Democratic Objectivecracy must know that one of the best tools for personal and societal improvement is debate. The debate tests the ideas and the arguments that support them. Debate enhances good ideas and dismisses weak or fallacious ideas. The citizen of a democratic objectivecracy must consider debate as the most honest tool to persuade and improve ideas and society. For these reasons, citizens must be accustomed and educated from childhood to debate and to develop their own criteria from a debate. Debates should be encouraged to resolve conflicts or make decisions in classrooms. Teachers in a school can use the debate, instead of the pulpit, to present different points of view to students.

In public debates, it should be mandatory for debaters to always show their sources and moderators should have the ability to fact check and to call out logical fallacies.

4) The thirst for knowledge.

Education and the operation of a Democratic Objectocracy should stimulate knowledge and make it clear to its members that without an adequate knowledge base they will hardly be able to make adequate decisions.

At this moment in our society, there is a great thirst for knowledge on topics such as the stories inside video games, comics, series, movies, celebrities, and sports. The human being loves and seeks knowledge. In a Democratic Objectivecracy, knowledge of public and social issues that affect the lives of citizens should be encouraged and facilitated.

5)   Argumentative logic.

In a Democratic Objectivecracy, it is vitally important that citizens get used to applying argumentative logic constantly during their lives so that when they are given political arguments, the citizen can use formal logic to evaluate them. The ability to detect fallacies will help citizens protect themselves against manipulation by powerful individuals, groups, or charlatans. At every level of the education process, argumentative logic must be thought and put into practice in increasingly complex situations. All members of a society must be able to identify arguments and fallacies.

6)   Identification and differentiation between facts, data, ideas, opinions, beliefs, feelings, and emotions.

For the optimal functioning of the Democratic Objectivecracy, it is of utmost importance that citizens know how to identify and differentiate between facts, data, ideas, thoughts, beliefs, feelings, and emotions. To achieve this, individual and group sessions of analysis, introspection, and analysis exercises should be organized and carried out from childhood. Because when people are not able to identify the difference between the previous concepts, they can be very easily manipulated by politicians, demagogues, powerful groups, advertising, and the media.

Currently, politicians and the media often combine partial data with opinions loaded with ideology that reinforce or go against the beliefs of citizens and generate strong feelings that are used to manipulate and achieve a political or economic objective.

7)   Transparency.

Society in general, from childhood, must be accustomed to being transparent and to demanding transparency from their institutions. The budgets of schools, classrooms, sports clubs, neighborhood associations, etc., and their expenses, must be open so that all members can see, question and perhaps improve them. Accustoming children and citizens to analyzing and seeking to improve budgets and expenses is very important.

The combination of the seven points above mentioned will help citizens take charge of their own life and society and to do so in a conscious, intentional, and rational way. This does not mean that this type of education must first be achieved in order for a Democratic Objectivecracy to be established. Because if human beings are deprived of their freedom on the excuse that they are not prepared to have it, they will never be prepared to have it. It is precisely the exercise of their freedom that makes human beings skilled in the exercise of their freedom. For a society to be free, the first requirement is that it has to be free. Only the use and application of their freedom can provide citizens with adequate experience and skill to make use of and expand their freedom. If a group or person considers that something is necessary before citizens can be free, it is oppressing them. By using freedom, by being free, individuals learn to be free and to use their freedom.

What do you think of the proposed education? Do you think it would be necessary to take more factors into account? Which? Do you think that the factors that need to be taken into account can be evaluated by citizens in their proposals and tenders?

____

____

____

____

CHAPTER 3

Physical Security

One of the basic objectives of every human society is physical security. That is, protecting people from violence, coercion, and physical force. It is not strictly necessary for a Democratic Objectivecracy to choose the security of its members as one of its objectives, but it is natural to assume that security will normally be one of the objectives of society.

Furthermore, if the society cannot provide physical security to its members, the members will be faced with the need to protect themselves. This has the following consequences:

1) Being a member of the society will not be attractive because it will not bring a basic benefit to its members.

2) The members of society will be obliged to protect their persons and interests through the use of force. This situation will accustom them to the use of force as a means to achieve their personal objectives; and that will lead to some members of society resorting to force and violence to oppress other members of society, thus dissolving the democracy.

3) The members of the society will find it necessary to form societies under the official society in order to protect themselves. These sub-societies will not necessarily function through the Democratic Objectivecracy system, or they will not be governed by the objectives and the system that governs the rest of the the society. This will generate sub-governments and sub-societies that

will undermine the democratic system in general and will have the potential to oppress the rest of the population.

It is up to each society governed by the Democratic Objectivecracy system to find the way in which they can protect their members, always taking care not to oppress them or to generate a police, judicial, or military force with the potential and power to oppress. Below I propose one way in which a security force within society can function. This is just one proposal and one of the many ways in which society can be organized to safeguard the physical safety of its members.

Proposal:

The security forces can be made up of five branches: Citizens in general, Citizen Guards, Response Forces, Investigators, and social workers.

1)   Citizens in general

At all times, each citizen has the power and responsibility to report a crime or an administrative offense. If a citizen witnesses a crime or administrative offense, he or she can collect video or audio evidence and/or call the citizen guards on duty, the response forces, investigators, or social workers.

To facilitate the above, a society can develop an application that all citizens can have on their cell phones, from where they can request assistance from the citizen guards on duty, the response forces, the investigators, or social workers; and where they can upload videos, photos, or audio that serve as evidence.

For example: If a citizen sees a badly parked car, they can take out their cell phone, open the application, take a photo of the car, its license plates, and the place where it is parked, and upload it to the system saying that it is a breach of the collective traffic contract.

If a citizen witnesses a violent act, from the application, he can issue an alert and request for the response forces to arrive.

2) The citizen guards

In addition to the fact that each citizen has the power to report and show evidence against someone who committed a crime or an administrative offense, citizens can also have the duty to dedicate some of their time to patrolling the streets and dedicating their time and full attention to helping other citizens, to making complaints, obtaining evidence of crimes and administrative misconducts and following up on citizen complaints.

If the members of a society decide they want to ask each other to dedicate some of their time and effort to social service, some of the citizens that have to do their social service can be designated to work as citizen guards.

The selection of citizens guards can be very similar to the selection of assembly members. From among all the people that have to give time for social service, young people in the age group of 23 to 26 and retirees of 60 to 70 years of age can be selected by lot to form squads of four citizen guards each, two young ones and two old retirees. These patrol groups could even be constituted of a young woman, a retiree, a young man, and a retiree.

This will allow citizens themselves to be in charge of security and will prevent abuses of power by the police forces. Each citizen protects and cares for his own community. In addition, both proposals will help to generate interaction between different members of society, to generate social cohesion, and citizen organization and participation.

Citizen guards do not respond to, or investigate, violent crimes. They are more akin to security guards, neighborhood watches, and first responders.

The first responsibility of the citizen guards is to devote 100% of their attention to helping other citizens and to denounce breaches of non-violent collective agreements. If the Citizen Guards detect or witness a violent act, they call the response forces; and if they witness an act that requires investigation, they call the investigators.

All citizens are trained to carry out their duties as citizen guards.

Everything citizen guards do is recorded and broadcast live to the network, to prevent abuse of power and to provide security.

When guards witness a violent crime or think there is a potential for a violent crime to develop, they have to call the response forces.

When the citizen guardian witnesses a crime or a non-violent administrative offense which requires a fine but does not require an investigation, they themselves can levy the fine or the warning.

When the citizen guardian witnesses a crime or a non-violent administrative offense that requires an investigation or to be brought to trial, they call the investigators who are dedicated to conducting the entire investigation and presenting the case to the courts.

When a citizen issues a security alert, the first to receive the alert are the citizen guards who have to get to the place where the alert was issued and, if it is a non-violent crime, take care of the necessary report and coordinate with investigators.

This social service can also be used as a justification to pay for college for the young and the pension of the retirees. If young people between the ages of 20 and 25 are asked to give one year of social service, and this service is used to serve as citizen guards and replace most of the police work, then society can reward these young people by paying their university fees. Likewise, if adults between the ages of 60 and 70 are asked to dedicate a year of their lives to social service, and this year of service they use to work with young people as citizen guards, society can reward these adults by paying their retirement pension.

3) The response force

They are citizens whose specific work is that of violent confrontation.

They may be members of companies that won the tender to do this job. If this is the case, the power that these companies have will have to be very consciously limited.

For example, each tendering company may consist of the equivalent of one SWAT team. In this way, there will be individuals trained and dedicated to the violent response, but they will not have a vertical and unifying hierarchical command. Each company may have five, ten, or fifteen members, but they are not a unified police force that can amass vast amounts of power and oppress society.

Ideally, in this case, each small company should be assigned a response area and they should be trained to coordinate with each other if they need to unite against a significant threat. When a citizen or citizen guard issues an alert of a violent crime, the team in charge of the area arrives to respond to the crisis. If the crisis is too violent, this team can ask for help from other response force teams.

At all times when the response forces are working, everything they do is recorded and uploaded to the web so that it can be monitored by citizens.

4) Investigators

The society's team of investigators are those who investigate and assemble criminal cases to be presented in court. These researchers may be part of companies and investigative agencies that win tenders, or be citizens who investigate individually. If this is the case, the citizens of the society will have to be careful not to give too much power to these companies and to review possible conflicts of interest.

Again, the ideal in this case is that there are multiple relatively small companies with the obligation to share all the information and be

100% transparent with each other and with the public. These companies can come together to investigate crimes that require a greater investigative force than each of them has separately.

The work of the investigation agencies can be divided; some of them can be dedicated only to the administrative offenses most commonly reported by citizens from their applications; others to non-violent crimes; others to corporate crimes; others to crimes of corruption; others to financial crimes, etc.

5)   Social Workers

Some problems or situations might be more than what a regular citizen guard team can handle but they might not require the force employed by the response team, or they might not be crimes that need investigators. For these situations, teams of available social workers are recommended. Individuals or small companies can tender to be the ones in charge of these situations. Every person, at any moment, should be able to ask for the assistance of social workers.

Each society must develop its own methods to guarantee the safety of its members; and to verify that these security forces do not have enough power to oppress a sector of society or all citizens. The above is just a proposal that maybe you can improve.

Do you think that it is possible that citizens can be in charge and responsible for their own safety? Do you think this could bring good results? Do you think this would be efficient? Do you think this would prevent corruption and oppression? Do you think the only way to achieve security is through a conventional police force? Do you think there may be other solutions? Do you think that these solutions can be reached through a Democratic Objectivecracy?

____

____

____

____

____

CHAPTER 4

Ready?

Throughout history, every time that a group of people or an idea attacks an oppressive status quo, intellectuals, oppressors, and even the oppressed, because through propaganda and manipulation the oppressed have often been convinced that the system actually benefits them, raise their voices with arguments against freedom and equality. The same will happen against the Democratic Objectivecracy and against any other proposal for a social system that strives to empower and expand the freedoms and opportunities of every human being.

Arguments against the Democratic Objectivecracy

Even before presenting these ideas to the public, I can imagine some of the arguments that will be used to attack the new social system.

1) The human being, the masses, are immoral, vicious, and cruel and therefore they will choose selfish, antisocial, unnatural, and oppressive objectives.

2) The masses are ignorant and unprepared to be free and rule themselves.

3) The system is very complicated. It will not work because it is a very complicated system.

Let us study and analyze these arguments:

1) The masses are immoral, vicious, and cruel and therefore they will choose selfish, antisocial, unnatural, and oppressive objectives.

The masses: the first thing that the person who argues in this way says is that he himself is outside the masses, that the masses are the others, and he is superior to these others that make up the masses. That he is one of the men of superior qualities and therefore he, or others who think like him, should govern without listening, without being democratic, without allowing the freedom of the masses. Against this single initial idea, we can apply all the arguments we gave against aristocracy, monarchy, and dictatorship.

The masses are immoral: this argument is very curious since, basically, it establishes that because the others are immoral, they do not deserve freedom and self-determination, and therefore they deserve to be oppressed. What this argument holds is that because the masses can be immoral, the moral people must commit the most immoral act of all, which is to oppress and deprive human beings of their freedom.

The masses will choose oppressive objectives: this means that because there is a possibility that the masses will decide to oppress, then they must be oppressed beforehand. To me, it seems that it is not the masses but those who do not consider themselves part of the masses who have the tendency to oppress. Although we must accept that usually if we take any one single person, or any group of people, and give him power, it is probable that he will start to consider himself the possessor of superior qualities and will start oppressing others; therefore, the entire system of the Democratic Objectivecracy is designed not to deposit too much power in a few hands and to avoid oppression.

If by oppression they mean limitation or elimination of the privileges of the few who oppress the many, of course they are right. The Democratic Objectivecracy seeks to remove the privileges of the oppressors and ensure circumstances in which not only a few but all have the opportunity to develop freely as human beings and to self-determination.

In a Democratic Objectivecracy, the objectives that reign are the midpoint of society; the average, where the different positions and ideas converge, not the tyranny of a minority over a majority or of a majority over a minority. It is the midpoint of society. So, it is a system that protects the citizens from the oppression of majorities or minorities.

2)   **Human beings are ignorant and unprepared to be free and to govern themselves.**

I think exactly the opposite. Those who throughout history have called themselves men of superior qualities, and in this case I use the word "men" with all its gender connotations because throughout history those who have declared themselves to be superior have mostly been men, and have affirmed that their superiority gives them the right or the responsibility to rule over others, have committed most of history's acts of oppression, violence, genocide, squandering, exploitation, and destruction. These men have instituted systems that oppress, exploit, and leave most of the world's populations in poverty. These superior men can be as intellectual as they want to be, but their intellectuality has not prepared them to be empathetic human beings who respect, promote, and expand the freedom, possibilities, and opportunities of their fellow human beings. In fact, we could affirm that superior men are not prepared to respect the freedom and humanity of all other human beings; therefore these superior men must be stopped from obtaining the power they will use to exploit and oppress other human beings.

Furthermore, even when we accept that certain human beings are more prepared to perform certain tasks and functions, no human being is more prepared than the other to decide what to do with their own life. To think that a human being can better know and decide what should happen to the life of another human being, is to reduce the human being to an object that we think should be controlled in the hands of another human being.

Freedom, responsibility, self-determination, collaboration, and organization are qualities that are strengthened when practiced and used constantly; they are not simple theories that can be learned in an abstract way. For the human being to be free and for him to be able to organize in a free society, he has to be free and he has to constantly use his freedom.

Against these arguments we can also apply the arguments we used against the monarchy, the aristocracy, the dictatorship, and the technocracy.

3) The system is very complicated. It will not work because it is very complicated.

In reality, it is not more complicated than the current system. Maybe it takes time for people to get used to it, but since the system allows and encourages citizen participation at all times, it will not only be a system but a way in which people will relate to each other and a way of viewing and living life.

Do you think that the Democratic Objectivecracy is a good system but that the human being or the current societies are not prepared for it? Why? What do you think is necessary for the human being to be prepared for a true democracy? How could we help prepare human beings to be truly free and live in a true democracy?

____

____

____

____

____

____

____

____

____

____

CHAPTER 5

Transition to a Democratic Objectivecracy

Anyone who wants freedom for himself and for other human beings, and wants to promote human development for himself and for others, should begin to ask himself: How can I help make our society more free and democratic? How can I help the evolution of society so that the next social change is achieved peacefully and not by violent means? How can I stop being an accomplice of the oppressive system?

Ask yourself these questions, think and use your rational capacity and creativity to discover ways by which you can help the evolution of the current system to a free and democratic one that can solve the problems that humanity is facing.

What have you thought? How can you stop being part of the oppressive system? How can you start making the transition to a truly democratic system, whether or not it is the Democratic Objectivecracy?

____

____

____

____

____

____

____

____

Interaction and Debate

The first step to start a change in society is to start talking, criticizing, and debating. This means to confront other human beings directly, to talk about ideas not just people or specific laws and politicians, to express and demonstrate through arguments that they are not free and that their society is not democratic; to talk about the Democratic Objectivecracy, to discuss different forms of social organization, and the possibilities of success they would have, etc.

The first and most necessary step to achieving true democracy, to expanding our freedoms, and to generating social cohesion is that we talk about these issues. We need to accept that we are polarized, that this does not benefit us, accept that we do not live in a democracy and that being in a democracy is, by far, more preferable than being in a dictatorship or one of the other more authoritarian systems of social organization.

Talk about these issues with your friends, debate them, maybe at first they will see you as a crazy person, but little by little, these ideas will be part of everyone's vocabulary. It will be normal to talk about a system change, not just about a president or governor change. Think, speak, criticise, discuss, listen, discern, propose, and act!

Write the names of the people or groups of people with whom you are going to talk about these issues:

____

____

____

____

____

____

____

____

____

____

____

____

Take power away from the elected politicians and distribute it among all citizens.

Right now, in our current political systems, we can think of ways to take power away from the politicians and to distribute that power among all citizens. For example, we can start by pressuring our governments and political parties to implement participatory budgeting first and then participatory fiscal policy.

The basic principle of participatory budgeting is that the citizens decide where to invest the government's money. The easiest way to do so is to let people choose their budget, not based on specific amounts of money but on percentages of the overall budget. This means that people do not need to decide to spend 1,000,000 USD on education, they need to decide what percentage of the budget that is available will be used on education. For example, you might think that from all the government's money at least 20% should go to education.

The process will be as follows:
1.   Every person has 100% of the budget to decide what to do with it.
2.   Every person writes a list of items where they want their government to spend their money.
3.   Every person assigns a percentage of the budget to each of the items on their lists.
4.   The items can be as generic or specific as they want them to be, with the knowledge that, generic items will be selected by more people, and specific items will be more isolated.
5.   The lists of every single person with their respective percentages are taken in and averaged to obtain the list of the whole society with the percentage of the budget that will be spent on each item. This generates the society's budget in a democratic and time-efficient way.

For example:
You might want your government to spend 30% of their budget on education, 10% on police and security, 15% on social services, 10% on environmental protection, 15% on military and international security, 10% on infrastructure, 10% on equitable economic development. On the other hand, one of your neighbors might want 30% on education, 30% on police and security, 30% on military and international services, 5% on social services, 5% on infrastructure. Yet another neighbor might want 40% on education, 10% on police and security, 20% on social services, 20% on environmental protection, 10% on the economic development of the underprivileged. If we average your budget proposal with those of both your neighbors the final budget will be: 33.3% for education, 16.6% on police and security, 13.3% on social services, 15% on military and international security, 10% on environmental protection, 5% on infrastructure, 3.3% on equitable economic development, and 3.3% on the economic development of the underprivileged.

How Participatory Fiscal Policy works.
There are many ways in which participatory fiscal policy might work and be put into practice.

Taxation policy is usually compromised of income taxes, capital taxes, consumption taxes, property taxes, estate taxes, and international trade tariffs.

A comprehensive way to handle the tax policy decisions to the citizens would be to address each and every one of these types of taxes individually and divide each one in a comprehensive way.

For example, we can take income taxes and divide the income levels of society in 10. The lower-income people in society will be at level 1 and the highest paid people in society will be at level 10. The citizens will be able to see the range in income that each income level has. For example income level 1 might earn from $0 to $1,000 each month. Every citizen in the country will give an amount that they think should be taxed to this income level. The answers from every citizen are averaged to generate the final answer of what the society as a whole thinks should be the take on people earning from $0 to $1,000 monthly. If our society is compromised of 10 people and 9 of them choose 0% taxes on income level 1, and 1 person chooses 10% taxes on income level 1, then the average will be 1% tax on people earning from $0 to $1,000 monthly. The same process applies to every other income level.

The citizens themselves get to decide individually what the taxation should be for every income level, and the answer every individual assigned to each income level is averaged to obtain the society's decision of what the tax on that income level should be.

This will be the most effective if the citizens can view in real-time how the tax they are proposing will affect the income of every level. For example, if the citizens have to decide the income taxes for the highest earners, they should be able to see that this group is compromised of around 10,000 people and that their income ranges from $1,000,000 to $100,000,000 monthly. A person might decide that they should pay 40% in taxes, so they will be able to see that this group will now earn from $600,000 to $60,000,000.

In essence, this is what participatory fiscal policy looks like. And the same principle applies to every other type of tax.

Products are divided into categories, from necessary to luxurious, the citizens can individually decide how much to tax each category and the answers that are assigned to each category are averaged to obtain the tax on each category of products.

Participatory budgeting and fiscal policy are not democratic objectivecracy, but it is a step towards it.

Both these proposals take power away from the politicians and distribute it among all the citizens. Both these proposals can be implemented while the current representative system is working and can be some of the first steps to change the whole system. First, take the power of the politicians to decide what to do with the government's money, and give that power to the people. Then take the politicians' power to decide the taxes, and give that power to the people. Once we have managed these, citizens will be one step away from deciding the objectives of the society.
If you want to know more about participatory budgeting and fiscal policy you can read the book: The Democratic Economy of an Objectivecracy, or you can visit the webpage: www.wejustcoop.org where you will find a brief explanation and projects intended to help transition our current political system to a more democratic one.

The Path to Democratic Objectivecracy

To put into practice, even on a small scale in small societies, the Democratic Objectivecracy principles or any of the other real democratic principles, will help us get used to being heard, being free, and being democratic. And when we get a taste of real freedom and power, we will naturally want to scale up the systems that give us a voice and freedom to higher levels until we modify the political systems that govern us. Maybe this year you are not going to get your whole country organized under the Democratic Objectivecracy system, but you can manage to form or change a small society; a neighborhood administration, a school, a club, an activity with friends, a cooperative, a union, a political party, a community, a municipality ... and eventually we will manage to change entire countries until the whole world is part of a confederation of confederations that is organized under the Democratic Objectivecracy system.

Neighbors

There are millions of neighborhood associations around the world that manage neighborhoods, condominiums, or apartment buildings. The Democratic Objectivecracy, or at least part of it, can be put into practice in these associations.

For example, in a neighborhood all the residents can choose their objectives and averaging everyone's objectives would determine the neighborhoods objectives. The residents can then propose projects or solutions. A committee selected by lottery, or the whole neighborhood, can then vote to choose the project or solution that they like the most and present the projects or conclusions to be implemented to the other neighbors. Members can veto the project or allow it to be carried out.

Clubs

There are millions of private clubs around the world, sports clubs, social, literary, scientific, intellectual, video game lovers, movie lovers, anime lovers, etc. In all these clubs, the Democratic Objectivecracy can be put into practice in the same way that it can be done with neighbors:

For example:

1) The Democratic Average Objectivecracy is used to choose the objectives of the club.
2) Club members develop proposals to achieve the club's objectives.
3) A committee is chosen by lottery.
4) Committee members evaluate the proposals submitted by other club members and choose among them.
5) The committee will present their selection to all club members and explain why they chose such projects to achieve the club's objectives.
6) The members of the club have the possibility to veto the proposal or approve it.
7) Some proposals are approved and carried out.

Social organizations, activists, and volunteers

Just as it can be done with neighborhoods and clubs, it is possible to organize an NGO or a society of activists and volunteers through the Democratic Objectivecracy system. It is my opinion that if an organization is committed to human development and freedom, then the NGO has the opportunity to put into practice and demonstrate how real democratic principles work within the organization itself. Otherwise, part of what the organization is doing is to maintain the status quo by continuing to ask their people to respect vertical and totalitarian authority.

Social Organizations, it is time to be democratic. Social organizations, if you are truly committed to freedom and human development, if you want to be part of the social evolution, be democratic, help promote democracy, and accustom people to being free and empowered.

In schools and universities

Many schools and universities function as places of "training" and conditioning, not of human development. Many schools and universities preach, transmit, and indoctrinate conformity to the rules, reverence to authority, confirmation of the status quo, elimination of an independent spirit, and indoctrination and inner conditioning to replace personal identity with invented, superficial and chauvinistic identities such as nationalism, classism, racism, alma mater pride, machismo, etc.

Parents, educators, teachers, school and university directors, if you want your children to develop freely and not submit; if you want the next generations to be free and not programmed and conditioned; if you want to help social evolution, use and accustom your children and students to use the real democratic principles in their school; promote debate, question authority, strengthen learning and the use of argumentative logic. Make each classroom a society, each generation a confederation, the entire school a confederation. Let the students debate about and choose the electives that will be available, the types of sports that will be available, the school colors, the school fair, school trips, the uniform or the lack of, food in the cafeteria, etc.

Teachers, do not train soldiers for the system, instead help the human development of free people.

In Families

Parents, encourage personal responsibility in your children; the ability to make decisions; to form their own personal criteria; encourage and empower your children to modify their own circumstances.

Choose issues and topics in which the family will function as a Democratic Objectivecracy or through direct democracy. Maybe the holidays, a remodel, the restaurant where they will eat on the weekend, the movie they will go to see at the movies, the menu one day a week. Seek, think, be creative. Do not train your children to be obedient, to follow authority, to kill themselves to be accepted. Answer their questions, debate with them, answer their "and why" questions, encourage and celebrate their individuality, their judgment, their knowledge, their voice, their decisions, and their freedom, and have them experience responsibility and consequences.

In groups of friends

Friends, or at least you who are convinced, put into practice the principles of Democratic Objectivecracy or direct democracy in your group of friends. Use your creativity and your brain power to develop ways in which you can apply democratic principles with your friends, to help and get them used to using the democratic process, making their voices heard through debate, having all the same values, and the same power.

Political Parties

Political Parties, politicians, lawyers, aspiring politicians, it is time to evolve. If we do not, heads will roll or we will die in the revolutions or dictatorships that the current system will generate. Create new parties that function internally with the system of the Democratic Objectivecracy and, although they cannot change the system in a single election, they can promise their voters that, if elected, they will not govern or legislate according to their personal principles, but rather, they will generate a democratic system on the side of the official system to take all the decisions, and to start changing the current system to a Democratic Objectivecracy. Once elected, organize an Objective election among all citizens, not just those who voted for you. Ask citizens for proposals on how to achieve your objectives. Choose from among them and give your citizens the option to issue a veto. Be 100% transparent, carry out and justify all your actions according to the scale of objectives. Doing this will accustom your citizens to being democratic, it will open precedents, and you will be in the public eye for being one of the first to change the system to a more democratic one. Be part of the vanguard of the change of the social system, of the movement of history towards a new form of social organization.

Referendums

Politicians, governors, if you are really democratic, at the very least change the way in which you do referendums, make use of the system proposed by the Democratic Objectivecracy, see how it works, and experiment with it. Be a force that evolves our society, not another of the many politicians who promise and are hated and despised by all.

Citizens around the world, when politicians propose a referendum, do not be fooled and manipulated by those who present you with a "yes or no" option without explaining the implications and objectives of each decision. Demand more information in radio stations, in letters to the government, in demonstrations, in signed petitions, in newspaper notes, in articles published in newspapers and magazines, on social media, by any means you can. Demand that the referendum stop being a polarizing "yes or no" contest; demand a first vote where each one sets out their objectives related to the topic to be discussed; demand that an assembly of citizens elected by lot be formed, that they obtain proposals to solve the problem they face, that these proposals go according to the objectives chosen by all citizens, that they explain this proposal to citizens and then all citizens can vote to accept or veto the proposal of the assembly.

Citizens, do not let the transcendent questions that will affect your entire nation become a television game of "yes or no". Referendums and your government will control or influence the circumstances in which you live and develop. Take control of your own circumstances, demand a referendum through the system of the Democratic Objectivecracy, and do not allow yourself to be manipulated and polarized.

This system can work for topics such as: Brexit, the legalization of drugs, the legalization or not of prostitution, refugees, abortion, participation in a war, changing the constitution, changing the electoral system of a country, changing taxes, etc.

Workers Unions

Workers of the world have fought for more than 200 years against oppression, exploitation and for equality. Be free in your own organizations to regain the legitimacy and vitality that your parents or grandparents had. Do not be part of one more oppressive system, do not govern yourselves under the electoral representative system that generates oligarchs and leaders with power inside the union. Use the Democratic Objectivecracy system, revitalize, energize your members in this way. Let them know that they are listened to, let them know they are part of the system, let it be known that it is they and their objectives that move them, not just another boss.

After the death or abdication of a dictator

It is time for the fall of totalitarian regimes in the world. Dictators are dying, some by natural causes, others by bullets, and still others are exiled. Citizens and leaders of these nations, you have an unprecedented opportunity in your hands: set the example of how a truly free and democratic society can develop; institute a Democratic Objectivecracy. With this system, you will have legitimacy and stability. With this system, you can develop individually and collectively. You who start a new nation, you can become oppressors, or be liberators. Choose freedom for all, be an example to all.

Without the rule of law

And you, citizens who live without the rule of law, where the State, the government, is just one more of the oppressors who demand money in exchange for not attacking you, develop neighborhood councils, develop alternate governments, and parallel systems. A voluntary neighborhood society that works with the system of Democratic Objectivecracy and that is related to the other neighborhoods through confederations. Together, you can solve more problems than the State is solving for you right now.

Members of the 1% and the 10%

You have the economic power that gives you access to political and military power. If you make the effort, you can generate the political, social, economic, and environmental changes necessary to be able to have free societies that respect and promote free human development for all its members. You have the power to decide if we change and evolve peacefully or if there will be violent revolutions where many suffer, including you. The current system is oppressive, and it will either evolve to be more oppressive or a violent revolution will erupt.

Let's change the system in peaceful ways before that happens. Are you an oppressor or a liberator? Will you help the free development of all human beings? Will you help to expand the freedoms of every human being? Please do not maintain and support the oppressive system, don't be oppressors.

Citizens around the world

Don't wait for your politicians to willingly want to change the system. The current system benefits them so they must be pressured to change the entire system. The transition can be done gradually, but it can be done.

Find a way to gradually change parts of the current system of oppressive representation.

For example:

1) Demand that in addition to the election of representatives an election of objectives takes place, and demand that the representatives use the objectives as a guide and justification for all their actions.

2) Demand that one of the houses of legislators be chosen by lot from among the citizens. In other words, if your country has a chamber of legislators and a chamber of senators, ask that one of the two, or half of the members of both houses be chosen by lot.

This will diminish the power of politicians and the interests of the powerful.

3) Demand the formation of an Auditing Assembly of all the actions of the state and that the Assembly be composed of citizens chosen by lottery and have the budget and the power to hire researchers and experts.

4) Demand that the referendums stop being "yes or no" contests, but that a process of committees or assemblies of citizens elected by lot be carried out, or that a complete Democratic Objectivecracy process be carried out.

5) Demand the replacement of your president or prime minister by a committee or an assembly. Start to distribute power and stop the concentration of power in a few hands.

6) Little by little, take power away from politicians and destroy the hierarchy that oppresses them.

7) Demand the implementation of participatory budgeting and participatory fiscal policy.

8) Demand the disintegration of traditional police and have citizens be in charge of most police duties through community service, rewarding those citizens by paying their universities, debts, or pensions.

Protests

Right now, there are protests and calls for reform in the United States, France, Chile, Venezuela, Iran, Israel, Beirut, Belarus and in many other countries of the world. Citizens, you are already in the streets, you are already asking for a change, so ask for a real change, for the change of system to a Democratic Objectivecracy. Do not be satisfied with removing the president. In turn, do not change one ruler for another. Instead, change the system. Demand the introduction of assemblies of citizen legislators selected by lottery; demand the election of objectives of the whole of society; demand the formation of an Assembly of Auditors; demand the election of taxes and public spending by using the Average Democracy process so that each citizen chooses what he considers the taxes of each sector of the population should be and where they should be invested; or even, strive for the complete transformation of the whole social organization to a complete Democratic Objectivecracy.

You

You who read this, whoever you are, wherever you are, be part of the evolution before our time is up. Use your creativity to look for ways to implement the Democratic Objectivecracy processes in your life and in that of your society. Think: What groups am I part of? Could they be democratic? And if not: What new groups would I like to develop and make democratic? Or even, can I start a political party, or ask those who are there to change to start working according to one or all the processes of the Democratic Objectivecracy system? Think about it, use your intelligence, your creativity, be part of and push for evolution, do not be complicit in the oppression of human beings and the destruction of the planet. Take action!

What actions are you going to take to be free and make your society more just and free?

____

____

____

____

____

____

____

____

____

PD

By now we have already analyzed the oppressive aspects of Representative Democracy through elections, we studied alternative systems, and we generated a new proposal of a new system of political and social organization. We did this to affirm and expand the freedom of the human being; your right to decide why you belong to a society, and the objectives of this society; and your right to have an influence on the circumstances in which you live, develop, and face.

However, in addition to the problem of Electoral Representative Democracy, we have the problem of capitalism. In the book "The Democratic Economy of an Objectivecracy", we explore the problems that capitalism generates, alternatives to said system, and an integration of the social, political, and economic organization through the Democratic Objectivecracy.

I separate the two books because, although I consider that to achieve true freedom it is necessary to extend democracy to the economic system, I also think that even the strongest proponents of capitalism can see the benefit of changing the current system of political organization to a Democratic Objectivecracy. If your argument is that you want capitalism because you want freedom, then I think you can understand the value of exchanging the current political system for that of Democratic Objectivecracy. If you defend capitalism because you consider it a free system, then the logical conclusion is that you prefer Democratic Objectivecracy to Electoral Representative Democracy.

Either way, I invite you to read the book "The Democratic Economy of an Objectivecracy". In this book, I present a critique of the capitalist system from the perspective of freedom and I propose a way to organize the economy using the system of Democratic Objectivecracy and the process of Average Democracy.

If you are a lover of freedom, I also invite you to read the books "The Ethics of Ambiguity" by Simone De Beauvoir and "On Freedom" by John Stuart Mill.

Now I invite you to continue reading, keep thinking, keep analyzing and begin to talk about these issues with your friends and acquaintances, and to start to take action to change the system that oppresses you to one that allows you to be free and to develop a free society.

If you have any questions or comments, if you have ideas that can improve the system, if you want to help promote the ideas of the Democratic Objectivecracy, if you want to help translate the book into another language, if you think you can write a book where you expose in a more attractive way the principles of the Democratic Objectivecracy, or that you can write a book improving the ideas or arguments of the Democratic Objectivecracy, write to me and we can collaborate, or write the book yourself and we can publish it as part of the Democratic Objectivecracy collection, or even publish it yourself. The important thing is to debate and promote these ideas.

Contact me at: Objectivecracy@gmail.com or visit the web page www.wejustcoop.org to learn about the projects we are currently developing to transform the political system to a truly democratic one.

I want to collaborate with you in a democratic way. Do you want to do the same?
I want to expand my freedom, my opportunities, and possibilities through free collaboration with you and with all the other human beings in the world. Do you want the same?

More freedom, more opportunities, more possibilities, and more collaboration.

Humans around the world, help me to be free and I will help you to be free! Let's be free together! Let's collaborate freely! Let's build truly democratic and free societies!

Thank you!

Bibliography

1: Johnson, Paulo. (2019). TUCÍDIDES. Por la razón o la fuerza. Introducción, traducción y notas de Roberto Torretti. Santiago: Ediciones Tácitas-Colección. 2017, 249 pp.. Alpha: Revista de Artes, Letras y Filosofía. 293-294. 10.32735/S0718-22012018000470018 5.

2: Rod Hague; Martin Harrop (31 May 2013). Comparative Government and Politics: An Introduction. Macmillan International Higher Education. pp. 1–. ISBN 978-1-137-31786-5. Archived from the original on 7 July 2019. Retrieved 25 February 2018.

3: An operational definition of epigenetics, Shelley L. Berger, Tony Kouzarides, Ramin Shiekhattar, Ali Shilatifard, Genes Dev. 2009 Apr 1; 23(7): 781–783. doi: 10.1101/gad.1787609

4: Early childhood deprivation is associated with alterations in adult brain structure despite subsequent environmental enrichment, Nuria K. Mackes, Dennis Golm, Sagari Sarkar, Robert Kumsta, Michael Rutter, Graeme Fairchild, Mitul A. Mehta, Edmund J. S. Sonuga-Barke, on behalf of the ERA Young Adult Follow-up team, Proceedings of the National Academy of Sciences Jan 2020, 117 (1) 641-649; DOI: 10.1073/pnas.1911264116

5: De Liberación Nacional, E. Z. (1996, January 1). Cuarta Declaración de la Selva Lacandona. Retrieved April 11, 2020, from https://enlacezapatista.ezln.org.mx/1996/01/01/cuarta-declaracion-de-la-selva-lacandona/

6: Ferguson, J., & CHISHOLM, K. (1978). Political and social life in the Great Age of Athens. London: Ward Lock Educational.

7: Aristotle, Barnes, J., & Lane, M. S. (2016). Aristotles politics: writings from the complete works. Princeton, NJ: Princeton University Press.

8: Montesquieu, C. de S., & Carrithers, D. W. (1977). The spirit of laws: a compendium of the first English edition. Berkeley: University of California Press.

About the Author

I really think that it is unnecessary to talk about me, because I think that the ideas of the book are the ones that have to be consistent in themselves and they have to be sufficient by themselves without any author authority. It doesn't matter who gives the argument, as long as the argument is correct. Please consider and evaluate the ideas in the book, not the writer.

If you insist on knowing a little more about me, I will tell you a little bit of my story. I was raised in a very Catholic home and at the age of 14, I entered the minor seminary of the Legionaries of Christ to study to become a priest. At 16, I stopped believing in God and left the seminary. I studied Mechanical Engineering for two years at the Tecnológico de Monterrey while I struggled with my desire to be a "normal teenager" and, facing the existential anguish, nihilism, and depression that the loss of my faith and reason for existing generated in me. I decided to leave engineering school and become a filmmaker. I went to live in CDMX, where I received a lot of help from a couple of friends and where I faced other difficulties such as sexual harassment from a couple of producers and tv industry people. I worked as a model, extra, production assistant, assistant director, director, and producer of corporate videos, commercials, short films, large films, and small and independent films. I built two independent film and video production companies. I worked with NGOs and with a couple of politicians who I thought were good people but, little by little, I realized that they were corrupt.

While doing all this, I read and wrote my own philosophy, I continued looking for a reason, a meaning, to my existence and an objective metric to judge good and evil, the good life, and to be able to make decisions and be satisfied with my life. Eventually, my philosophical concern went from being something personal to being something social. Because one of the answers I gave to the question

"How can I live a life worth living?" is: being free and relating, collaborating, sharing with and loving free human beings.

In 2017, an earthquake shook central and southern Mexico. I enlisted to help with rescue efforts in small towns in the state of Morelos. There I faced a type of poverty that I had not faced before, sick people living in dirt houses. I remember that the roof of a family's house was a plastic tarp from a billboard advertisement for a political candidate. The only thing that politicians had done to help that community was to generate garbage with their campaign material that would later be used as construction material.

I reflected upon my life and the world and I decided to live the independent film production company that I had at that time. The next two-and-a-half years of my life I spent reading, reflecting, and writing. I decided to make many changes in my life and to develop the book that you now hold in your hands. Now I seek communities of free human beings and I seek to collaborate freely, love, experiment, live freely, build my life and, if possible, a free world. That is why I started the cooperative NGO: We Just Coop. If you like the ideas presented on this book, visit the page www.wejustcoop.org , maybe you will like some of the projects and many we can work on something together. We need all the brains we can get.

Dedication

Thank you, Grandfather Charro, because from you I learned to face and enjoy life.

Thank you Lore, because from you I learned to accept love, to grow, to explore myself, to be more myself, and to overcome myself.

Thanks Diego Gallegos, because I learned from you not to be afraid to show my love towards my male friends.

Thank you Sánchez Toro family, because from you I learned to give without expecting anything in return.

Thank you Cesar, for being my friend.

Thanks Mayagoitia, for the debates.

Thank you Javier Reynso, for your help.

Thank you Katy and Storm, for your smiles, your love and your encouragement.

Thank you Genaro, for the time we shared.

Thank you Leha, for helping me when I was alone.

Thanks Caty for your love, thanks Esteban for always supporting me, thanks Adry for motivating me, thanks Robe for sharing so much with me, thanks José for your friendship, thanks Mother for supporting me and correcting (the text), thanks Dad for opening the doors of your home and refrigerator during the Covid quarantine.

Thank you Storm and Katy for the wonderful friendship we share.

Thank you tripie for always being there.

Thank you all...

From everything I have learned everything, and from everything I am yet to learn everything.